GOD
IN THREE
PERSONS

E. Calvin Beisner

LIVING STUDIES
Tyndale House Publishers, Inc.
Wheaton, Illinois

All Scripture quotations are from the Holy Bible,
New International Version, copyright © 1978 by
New York International Bible Society

Library of Congress Catalog Card Number 84-51210
ISBN 0-8423-1073-8
Printed in the United States of America
    7   8   9   10   92   91   90

CONTENTS

PREFACE

Is the doctrine of the Trinity a man-made creed or is it truly a biblical doctrine? In this book we will see that the Nicene-Constantinopolitan Creed, though formulated by mere men, is an accurate representation of the teaching of the New Testament. In this work, we will examine the doctrine from four directions. (1) First, we will study the New Testament teaching on the doctrine of the Trinity which, though our study is not exhaustive, will show that the New Testament does teach such a doctrine. (2) We will also study *how* the doctrine of the Trinity was believed, up to the time that the Nicene-Constantinopolitan Creed was formulated. We will study the creeds, confessions, and general writings of the early Church Fathers. (3) We will look also at the Arian controversy of the fourth century, from which arose the original form of the Creed at the Council of Nicea, A.D. 325, and later in the second form sometime between A.D. 340 and 360, adopted at the Council of Constantinople, A.D. 381, proclaimed orthodox by the Council of Chalcedon, A.D. 450. (4) We will also look at the meaning of the later form (that which is more commonly thought of as the "Nicene Creed"), comparing its understanding of the doctrine of the Trinity with the teachings of the New Testament.

Certain things, though they might be expected in a full-length study of the development of the doctrine of the Trinity, will not be a part of this study. First, there is no comparison between the Christian doctrine of the Trinity and the many "trinities" of other religions and philosophies. Other studies have shown that such so-called parallel views of the Trinity are really not parallels at all, but are only outwardly similar.

It has also been impossible in this short study to present a complete study of all trinitarian development in the writings of the Church Fathers. I have, however, attempted to sketch at least the outlines of such development.

I have not attempted an in-depth view of the New Testament teaching of the doctrine of the Trinity. The reader who wishes to see a discussion of all verses traditionally related to this doctrine will do better to look in a systematic theology or a traditional defense of the doctrine. What I have attempted to do is to present the evidence for the doctrine from a few of the most important texts.

It has also been necessary to ignore what is referred to as the *filioque*, the doctrine that the Holy Spirit proceeds not only from the Father but also from the Son. This is a late addition to the Nicene Creed, accepted in the Western Church only. It is, with the doctrine of the infallibility of the pope and papal authority, one of the primary causes of division between East and West. This doctrine does not really pertain to the essential doctrine of the Trinity.

Readers who are familiar with higher critical approaches to the New Testament may be surprised at the lack of consideration which these theories and their implications receive in this discussion of the New Testament doctrine of the Trinity. This is not due to any ignorance of these theories. But since I believe that the New Testament (along with the Old) is the inspired Word of God and thus inerrant in its original writing, when I read in one of the Gospels that Jesus said something, I believe that the historical person, Jesus Christ of Nazareth, said it, not that it is a product of the early Church.

I offer this work in the hope that it might prove interesting and informative, and with the humble prayer that it may be pleasing in the sight of God.

INTRODUCTION

My interest in Christianity comes primarily because it is my faith. It is fascinating to know that the faith of a Christian is both a highly personal, subjective affair, and also a powerful intellectual system which is open to scrutiny from all quarters as an objective set of beliefs. There is a distinction to be made, however. It would be wrong to think that the faith of an individual Christian is "the faith" of Christianity. However, if one wishes to be "Christian," it seems only reasonable that he should believe at least the essential parts of the Christian faith, which we will discuss later.

In asking the questions of what the Christian faith is and what it is not, I have noticed two very important facts. First, within "the faith" of Christianity there is wide latitude for disagreement over many matters. Second, there is also a definite dividing line between what is Christian and what is not.

The dividing line between "the faith" of Christianity and faiths which are not Christian is a line built of doctrines—doctrines which are essential to the faith. These doctrines have been expressed throughout the history of Christianity in different ways, ranging from the explicit and highly technical language of the so-called "Athanasian Creed" (early fifth century A.D.) to the simple, yet profound language of Peter in saying to Jesus, "You are the Christ, the Son of the living God" (Matt. 16:16, NIV). This statement by Peter forms what may be the earliest semiofficial confession of faith or creed. The Athanasian Creed is one of the most precise statements of the essentials of the Christian faith, and dwells on the doctrine of the Trinity.

> . . . the Catholic Faith is this: That we worship one God in Trinity, and Trinity in Unity; Neither confounding the Persons: nor dividing the Substance [Essence]. For there is one Person of the Father: another of the Son: and another of the Holy Ghost. But the Godhead of the Father, of the Son, and of the Holy Ghost, is all one: the Glory equal, the Majesty coeternal. Such as the Father is: such is the Son: and such is the Holy Ghost. The Father uncreate [uncreated]: the Son uncreate [uncreated]: and the Holy Ghost uncreate [uncreated]. The Father incomprehensible [unlimited]: the Son incomprehensible [unlimited]: and the Holy Ghost incomprehensible [unlimited, or infinite]. The Father eternal: the Son eternal: and the Holy Ghost eternal. And yet they are not three eternals: but one eternal. As also there are not three uncreated: nor three incomprehensibles [infinites], but one uncreated: and one incomprehensible [infinite]. So likewise the Father is Almighty: the Son Almighty: and the Holy Ghost Almighty. And yet they are not three Almighties: but one Almighty. So the Father is God: the Son is God: and the Holy Ghost is God. And yet they are not three Gods: but one God. So likewise the Father is Lord: the Son is Lord: and the Holy Ghost Lord. And yet not three Lords: but one Lord. For like as we are compelled by the Christian verity: to acknowledge

every Person by himself to be God and Lord: So are we forbidden by the Catholic Religion: to say, There be [are] three Gods, or three Lords. The Father is made of none: neither created, nor begotten. The Son is of the Father alone: not made, nor created: but begotten. The Holy Ghost is of the Father and of the Son: neither made, nor created, nor begotten: but proceeding. So there is one Father, not three Fathers: one Son, not three Sons: one Holy Ghost, not three Holy Ghosts. And in this Trinity none is afore, or after another: none is greater, or less than another [there is nothing before, or after: nothing greater or less]. But the whole three Persons are coeternal, and coequal. So that in all things, as aforesaid: the Unity in Trinity, and the Trinity in Unity, is to be worshiped. He therefore that will be saved, must [let him] thus think of the Trinity.[1]

How does one proceed from the words "You are the Christ, the Son of the living God," to the detailed statement above? That is one of the questions of this book. The confession of Peter contains within it the implications, conscious and unconscious, in Peter's mind when he said it. Peter stood before one who was a man—a man of peculiar nobility, but a man all the same. Yet he said to him, "You are the Christ," the "Anointed One," the "Messiah" foretold in Hebrew Scripture.

This "Anointed One" was described in two primary ways in the Old Testament. The description more commonly thought of by the Jews of Peter's day was that of a King coming to release God's people from bondage and to usher in the reign of righteousness, the Kingdom of God on earth. The second conception was of One who would suffer a substitutionary death as a sacrifice for the sins of his people (Isa. 53).

13

Peter's subsequent actions before the death of Christ lead us to think that he probably had the first description in mind, though we cannot be sure. What we can know, however, is that his confession that Jesus was "the Christ" implied everything taught of the Messiah in the Old Testament. Later Christian teachings expounded on these concepts, and much of that interpretation is available to us in the New Testament.

The second point which Peter stated is more surprising when we remember that he said it to a man: "You are the Christ, the Son of the living God." The implications here are tremendous for Christology from the first century through the present. We can see one implication of this when we compare it with what the Jews concluded regarding Jesus when he claimed that God was his Father. We are told in John (5:18) that in response to this claim the Jews attempted to stone Jesus, because, in John's words, "he was . . . calling God his own Father, making himself equal with God." That the term "Son of God" meant to a Jew "equal with God" may be assumed from the common reaction of the Jews, both in this instance and in that recorded in John 10:36-39. The Jews believed that everything reproduced after its own kind, that is, brought forth offspring having the same nature as the parent (Gen. 1:21). For Peter to call Jesus "the Son of the living God," therefore, almost certainly means that Peter thought of Jesus as having the same nature as God.

It is this latter factor, the nature of Jesus as "Son of God," which became the center of trinitarian controversy for centuries to come; and it is this which evolved, over a period of roughly five hundred years, into the kernel of the Athanasian Creed. (The statements about the Holy Spirit evolved more slowly but along parallel lines.)

We can see, however, the beginning of the trek from "You are the Christ, the Son of the living God," to the

14

detailed statement in the Athanasian Creed. The development occurred in four ways.

First, Christians wished to find ways to express briefly and succinctly, yet without imprecision or inaccuracy, what they taught about Christ and the rest of the faith. These expressions began to turn into "creeds." "Creed" comes from the Latin *credo*, "I believe," which was often the first word in a confession of faith.

In the Eastern Church the confession was usually a πιστεύομεν or *credimus*, "we believe," making the creed a corporate confession of the body of the Church, while the Western Church used πιστεύω or *credo*, "I believe," making it a personal confession.

The desire to express the teaching of Scripture briefly led to the formulation of the creeds. These creeds were often used as catechetical tools, and assent to a short creed was usually required of new converts before their baptism.

Second, creeds developed as ways of expressing what Christians experienced. Unlike pure philosophical discussion, the creeds invariably had to do with the heart of the experience of Christians. They were not formulated for the sake of intellectual stimulation or exercise, but to explain why Christians experienced one thing and not another in their social and spiritual lives.

Third, creeds were formed for the purpose of making known to prospective converts precisely what Christianity believed and taught, so that they could make informed decisions. Confessions of faith, creeds, or symbols, three terms for virtually the same thing, formed the basis of catechesis from the earliest times of Christianity.

Fourth, creeds were formed in order to combat what Christians thought was error. This was the most powerful stimulant to the development of the creeds by the early Christians. They were convinced that certain teachings called Christian were contrary to the teaching of Christ and the apostles. For this reason, councils met and creeds were formed not so much to preserve unity as to defend truth. The New Testament itself contains material combatting pseudo-Christian errors. Paul and John combatted gnosticism in two of their letters (Colossians and 1 John). Paul fought legalism in Galatians, and the author of Hebrews argued against a Judaizing tendency.

We are often told that the only thing we learn from history is that we never learn anything from history. It certainly does seem that some people never learn from history, and go on making the same mistakes over and over. But more likely everyone can learn at least something from history. It is particularly with this fact in mind that this book is written.

The Christian Church exists today in a civilization which undergoes vast changes at rapid speeds. In our age of instant communication and nearly-instant transportation around the world, religious ideas are being exchanged with ever-increasing frequency and openness, which brings with it blessings and dangers.

What we are seeing is a modern repetition of many of the belief systems which were combatted in the early centuries of Christianity. Old doctrines surface with new names and faces, and "there is no new thing under the sun" (Eccl. 1:9). The Christian Church must learn from its past if it is to recognize these teachings as they spring up. We have much to gain from our predecessors in the faith, who have in many instances already confronted the many doctrines now challenging the faith.

Working in the field of the Christian and non-Christian cults for five years, I have studied dozens of religious groups which call themselves Christian but which deviate in some way from the Christian faith. I have not yet seen one which brings with it a system of doctrine not found in whole or in part in one or more

16

of the schismatic sects of the first four or five centuries of Christianity.

Three schismatic positions are the most commonly adopted. First is Arianism, or what we know today as Unitarianism. This system has as its chief cornerstone the denial of the true deity of Jesus Christ. The name Arianism stems from its proponent in the fourth century, Arius of Alexandria (d. 336). Arianism has surfaced again and again in the history of the Church, having been taught by Servetus, Socinus, and in the nineteenth century by the Unitarians and others.

The second position is gnosticism, the heart of which is the belief that matter is either evil or nonexistent. The name comes from the Greek γνῶσις, "knowledge," and was adopted because those teaching this professed a special hidden knowledge above that available to most people. Its chief denial of Christian faith had to do with denying the actual incarnation of the Word, the Son of God, for in believing that matter is evil or nonexistent, it was thought necessary that the pure Word or λόγος of God could not come into such union with it as is taught in the doctrine of the incarnation.

The third position is Monarchianism, which laid such stress on the oneness of the deity that it could admit no personal distinctions within it. The name comes from the Greek μοναρχία. Monarchianism took two forms: dynamic Monarchianism and modalistic Monarchianism. Dynamic Monarchianism held that the man Jesus was born just as all others are born, and was at a later time adjudged righteous enough that he should be given a special portion of the divine nature. The teaching assumed many forms and had many refinements. Modalistic Monarchianism held that the Father, Son, and Holy Spirit spoken of in the New Testament were different modes in which the one Person of the divine monad revealed himself to and related

17

to man. Thus the Father actually was the Son, and the Son actually was the Holy Spirit.

It was chiefly against Arianism that the Nicene-Constantinopolitan Creed was formulated. Gnosticism was largely answered in the New Testament itself and by the Fathers of the second and early third centuries. Monarchianism in its respective forms was answered primarily by the Fathers of the third centuries (especially Hippolytus against modalism, and Tertullian against dynamic Monarchianism).

Arianism, gnosticism, and Monarchianism are represented today by several groups. The Jehovah's Witnesses and their dozen or more spin-off groups; the Worldwide Church of God, founded by Herbert W. Armstrong; the Concordant Publishing Concern; Christadelphianism, and the many types of Unitarianism all teach Arian theology.

Christian Science, Religious Science, the so-called "mind sciences," and a number of eastern groups incorporating some Christian terminology and ideas, such as the Theosophical Society, are modern representatives of gnosticism.

Monarchianism is represented today by the United ("Jesus Only") Pentecostals and by the small sect which calls itself the "Local Church," led by Witness Lee. As the differences between modalism and pure trinitarianism are rather minute, it is not surprising that a great number of Christians in mainline denominations, including Roman Catholicism, hold a modalistic conception of the Trinity, at least unconsciously.

There was, of course, one further position regarding the relation between Christ and God the Father in the early Church: polytheism. This, however, was quite rare. Rather than any one group actually teaching polytheism, certain groups accused each other of teaching it. The modalists would accuse trinitarians of polytheism for distinguishing the persons of the Trinity from each other. The Arians leveled the same charge against the orthodox parties. The orthodox trinitarians, on the other hand, accused the Arians of polytheism because the Arians called the Son a second God, created by the Father. Today, however, there is one schismatic group from Christianity which clearly does teach polytheism, the Church of Jesus Christ of Latter-day Saints, or Mormons.

What, then, is the dividing line between the Christian faith and that which is pseudo-Christian or openly non-Christian? The line must be drawn based on the identity of the person and work of Jesus Christ, for it is his person on whom the Church is built (1 Pet. 2:5-10; Eph. 2:20-22), and it is his work which forms the core of the gospel (1 Cor. 15:1-7). It is he who said, "I am the way and the truth and the life. No one comes to the Father except through me" (John 14:6).

The Christian Church throughout history has found that in order to remain faithful to the teaching of the New Testament regarding the person and work of Christ, it had to affirm at least the following doctrines: (1) The doctrine of the Trinity—that in the nature of the one true God, there are three distinct persons, the Father, the Son, and the Holy Spirit, each fully God, coequal and coeternal. (2) The doctrine of the incarnation—that the Son of God, the Word (John 1:1) became man (John 1:14; Rom. 1:3), uniting in the single person of the Son two distinct and complete natures, deity and humanity. (3) The sinless life of Christ—that he lived as the perfect man to fulfill God's plan for all humanity (Heb. 2:6-18; 4:14, 15); (4) The sacrificial death of Christ—to atone for the sins of all men (1 John 2:2; 1 Pet. 2:24; Matt. 20:28), and purchase the salvation of believers (Acts 20:28; 1 Cor. 6:20). (5) The resurrection of Christ—that after his death, Christ rose bodily from the grave, showing his triumph over sin and death, as the firstfruit, and hence the promise, of resurrection to all who have faith in him (1 Cor. 15; Rom. 6:3-11). (6) Salvation by grace through faith—that justification before God, and hence salvation from punishment and life with God, are available only as a gift from God through faith in Jesus Christ (John 14:6; 3:16; Acts 4:10-12; John 8:24).

Certain other doctrines, such as the virgin birth and those relative to the nature of man, heaven, and hell, and the inspiration and authority of the Bible, are related to these doctrines more or less directly. That of the virgin birth is essential as related to the sinlessness of Christ, granted the doctrine of original sin; that of the creatureliness of man and his sinfulness are related to the work of Christ, in that man stands in need of salvation; and to the person of Christ, in that Christ alone among men is the Mediator between God and man (1 Tim. 2:5), as the unique Son of God incarnate.

It is with the doctrine of the Trinity exclusively that this book is concerned, and comments on other doctrines will be made only as they relate to points being considered.

I

THE DOCTRINE OF THE TRINITY IN THE NEW TESTAMENT

THE first source to which Christian theology looks for its teachings is the New Testament. It is the New Testament which unfolds the divine plan introduced in the Old, and it is by the New Testament revelation that the Old Testament revelation is interpreted. For this reason all Christian theologians, orthodox and unorthodox, at least until near the end of the nineteenth century, have made the New Testament their primary source for data in constructing views of God and his relation to the world.

It is to this source, then, that we must first turn in attempting to understand later Christian trinitarianism. The Church Fathers consistently turned to it to formulate their doctrines of the Trinity; and in this chapter we will try to trace for ourselves, in our own way, the clues which they thought led inexorably to a doctrine of the Trinity.

It is necessary, of course, to come to a definition of that for which we seek. The Nicene Creed, in its form after the Council of Constantinople (A.D. 381), stated it as follows:

> I believe in one God the Father Almighty; Maker of heaven and earth, and of all things visible and invisible. And in one Lord Jesus Christ, the only-begotten Son of God, begotten of the Father before all worlds, God of God, Light of Light, true God of true God, begotten, not made, being of one substance with the Father; by Whom all things were made; . . . And in the Holy Ghost, the Lord and Giver of life; who proceedeth from the Father; who with the Father and the Son together is worshiped and glorified.

The essence of this statement is that there is one God who is a being composed of three individuals, the Father, the Son, and the Holy Spirit, all of whom are to be worshiped as the same God, and who share in the same substance or essence.

We may condense this into a somewhat shorter statement, one which is more precise: In the nature (or substance) of the one true God, there are three distinct persons, the Father, the Son, and the Holy Spirit. Here is the primary idea of a "tri-unity," a "Trinity in unity," three persons sharing equally in a single substance of deity.

The question to be asked here is: Does the New Testament contain such a doctrine, either explicitly or implicitly? And the question which follows is: If so, how does it?

The answers given by scholars to both these questions are, to say the least, widely variant. Some would contend that the doctrine of the Trinity is one of the most plain teachings of the New Testament, and even that it can be proved (not merely seen to be intimated) in the Old. Others go to the other extreme and argue that there is no such thing as a doctrine of the Trinity in either Testament, either in word or in thought, and that the doctrine of the Trinity itself is completely contrary to biblical and Judeo-Christian thought of the first century. We can see some of the divergencies of opinion when we approach the various writers on the subject.

K. E. Kirk, writing in his essay, "The Evolution of the Doctrine of the Trinity,"[1] said,

> The evidence of the New Testament is singularly disconcerting. Read in the light of the later faith of the Church, it presents an almost explicit Trinitarianism. Read apart from that light—as modern theology attempts to read it—it presents an almost inextricable confusion of ideas. . . .to us it appears that this is due not to a slow but essentially unilinear development of the doctrine, but rather to a struggle between a binitarian and trinitarian interpretation of the Christian facts—a struggle which maintained itself for nearly four centuries.

On the other hand, Augustus Strong quoted a long statement by the nineteenth-century Unitarian leader George E. Ellis,[2] who says in substance that the orthodox conception of doctrine, particularly of the doctrine of the Trinity, is so plainly taught in Scripture that the only reasonable escape from it for Unitarians is to deny the authority of the New Testament itself, for "Only that kind of ingenious, special, discriminative, and in candor I must add, forced treatment, which it receives from us liberals can make the book teach anything but Orthodoxy." According to Reverend Ellis, if it be granted that the New Testament is authoritative, then it must be granted that the orthodox position is authoritative, for "its obvious sense, its natural meaning" yield only the Orthodox creed.

The position which we must take is one which is in substantial agreement with that of Ellis, but which is, I think, somewhat more reserved. With Dr. Benjamin

Warfield[3] I conclude that "... the doctrine of the Trinity lies in the New Testament rather in the form of allusions than in express teaching ... is rather everywhere presupposed, coming only here and there into incidental expression, than formally inculcated." It seems that in reality the doctrine of the Trinity is that which is necessary to make sense of the New Testament statements regarding God the Father, the Son, and the Holy Spirit, and their relations to each other and to men, rather than that which is openly taught and advocated by the New Testament.

We may break the doctrine down into four parts for study in the New Testament. (1) The first point in the doctrine is that of unity, that there is one and only one true God. (2) The second is that there is a person called the Father, who is also called God. (3) Third, there is a person called the Son, or Christ, who is called God. (4) Fourth, there is a person called the Holy Spirit who is called God. It need only be added that the first point is, as it were, an umbrella over the other three, so that we will not fall into the erroneous view of the three names standing merely for different relations of one person to the creation. That is, the three persons of the Trinity are really three persons, and really one God.

MONOTHEISM IN THE NEW TESTAMENT

That the New Testament is monotheistic at the core is a fact recognized generally on all sides. The shadow of the *Shema*, "Hear O Israel: The Lord our God is one Lord" (Deut. 6:4), though never quoted in the New Testament (though alluded to in James 2:19), broods over its pages with all the weight it carried in Old Testament times, being the chief and holiest declaration of the Jewish religion. Such a monotheistic view pervades the whole outlook of Jesus: "It is written:

'Worship the Lord your God and serve him only'" (Luke 4:8). He prayed to his Father, "Now this is eternal life: that they may know you, the only true God, and Jesus Christ, whom you have sent" (John 17:3).

While Christ assumed monotheism from the start, the Apostle Paul specifically set about to answer the question whether there are more gods than one: "So then, about eating meat sacrificed to idols: We know that an idol is nothing at all in the world and that there is no God but one. For even if there are so-called gods, whether in heaven or on earth (as indeed there are many 'gods' and many 'lords'), yet for us there is but one God, the Father, from whom all things came and for whom we live; and there is but one Lord, Jesus Christ, through whom all things came and through whom we live" (1 Cor. 8:4-6).

The answer for Paul was that "there is no God but one," although there are those which are called gods. The reason is that the ones who are called gods "by nature are not gods" (Gal. 4:8). This monotheistic viewpoint rules the whole New Testament, but is nowhere more strongly stated than here in the writings of Paul. All others are demigods, "gods" in name only, unworthy of any sort of respect or worship. There is "one God and one mediator between God and men, the man Christ Jesus" (1 Tim. 2:5). In what may have been an early doxology among Christians, Paul wrote, "Now to the King eternal, immortal, invisible, the only God, be honor and glory for ever and ever. Amen" (1 Tim. 1:17).

THE FATHER IN THE NEW TESTAMENT

The fact that the New Testament teaches the deity of the "Father" is so well known as to be a truism. Yet there is one matter to which we must give attention.

There are three senses, it appears, in which "Father" is used in the New Testament in relation to God: (1) A Hebraism, common also in other religions, in which God is spoken of as the "Father" in the sense that he is Creator of all. (2) A parabolic sense of the word, very common in Jesus' teachings, in which "Father" is not intended to denote a distinct person in the Godhead, nor the fact of the creatorship of God, but the relation of God to the world or to individuals as "father" to children. This sense is often confused with the third sense: (3) A sense of the word in which it is clearly designed to refer to a specific individual personality, a technical term distinguishing the Father in the Godhead, in his internal relations, from the Son.

It is this third sense of the term "Father" in which we are here interested. Do we find, in the New Testament, an individual person who is called "the Father," in this sense of distinguishing him from "the Son," who is said to be God? There can be no doubt that we do. One of the plainest examples is the famous "high-priestly prayer" of Christ (John 17), which he begins by praying, "Father, the time has come. Glorify your Son, that your Son may glorify you. For you granted him authority over all men that he might give eternal life to all those you have given to him. Now this is eternal life: that they may know you, the only true God, and Jesus Christ, whom you have sent." The alternation between "Father" and "Son" here is clearly more than merely parabolic. It is the inner conversation of one individual with another, a communion most intimate and unique, and which is necessary to distinguish the Father from the Son in the Godhead. Here we have not only the distinction of Father and Son drawn for us, but also the statement of the deity of the Father: "that they may know you, the only true God."

28

The rest of the New Testament agrees with this. We find deity expressly attributed to "the Father" in Philippians 2:11 and 1 Peter 1:2, among other places. We saw Paul writing of "one God, the Father" (1 Cor. 8:6), and in 1 Corinthians 11:3 we see the Father referred to, granted without using the name, as the "head" of Christ, that is, "God." In all these places the Father is set in relation to his Son, Jesus Christ, and it is clear in each case that the reference is neither to "the Father" simply as Creator nor to the "the Father" in the parabolic sense, but to "the Father" as an individual in relation to another individual, Jesus Christ "the Son."

THE SON IN THE NEW TESTAMENT

When we approach the subject of the deity of Christ in the New Testament, we reach a point at which there is again division among scholars. There is no doubt that the writings of John hold the Son to be God (John 1:1; 5:18; 8:58; 20:28; Rev. 22:7-16), but many scholars would explain this as a late addition to Christian thought which had no place in the early Church, and found its way into the New Testament through the writings of one who was mistakenly identified by later Christians with the Apostle John. The argument is often advanced that the early writings of the New Testament, which represent the real beliefs of the earliest Church, and hence are closest to the actual teachings of Jesus, do not in any way present Christ as God. Some suggest that even the Apostle Paul did not identify Jesus as God.

It is amazing that anyone could attribute this view to Paul, for there are several instances in which Paul expressly used θεός of Christ in the absolute sense. Paul wrote, "Theirs [the Jews'] are the patriarchs, and from them is traced the human ancestry of Christ, who is

God over all, forever praised! Amen" (Rom. 9:5). Although the older translations often placed a period between "Christ" and the phrase "God over all," making the last phrase a doxology, it is clear from recent studies that this should not be done, and that the correct translation shows "God" as referring to Christ.

Paul's words in Acts were: "Be shepherds of the church of God, which he bought with his own blood" (Acts 20:28). There can be no questioning the reference to Christ here. It is Christ who "died for the ungodly" (Rom. 5:6), whose blood was shed for sinners, and which is the purchase of the Church of God.

Titus 2:13 is another instance in which earlier translations obscured the true meaning of the Greek. The *New International Version*, along with certain other newer versions, gives the correct rendering: ". . .we wait for the blessed hope—the glorious appearing of our great God and Savior, Jesus Christ." It is, in fact, in this context also that Paul connected Christ's being God with his purchasing the Church: "who gave himself for us to redeem us from all wickedness and to purify for himself a people that are his very own, eager to do what is good" (Tit. 2:14). Both here and in Acts 20:28 Paul connected the deity of Christ with the redemption effected by his death.

As if the fact that Paul called Christ θεός were not enough, we have even in the very passage in which Paul speaks of the *kenosis* of Christ, the "emptying" which Christ effected in being incarnated, a statement of Christ's abiding deity. In Philippians 2:6 and 7, Paul wrote of Christ, "Who, being in very nature God, did not consider equality with God something to be grasped, but made himself nothing, taking the very nature of a servant, being made in human likeness." The Greek phrase here translated "being in very nature God" could be translated literally "continuing to subsist in the form of God."

R.C. Trench shows that the deity of Christ is affirmed by the phrase "in the form of God":

> The μορφή then, it may be assumed, is of the essence of a thing. We cannot conceive the thing as apart from this its formality, to use 'formality' in the old logical sense; . . .[4]

We have in Philippians 2:6-11, then, a remarkable testimony of Paul on the deity of Christ, balanced perfectly by one of the strongest testimonies to Christ's full and complete humanity. Indeed, Paul ended the passage by applying to Christ a passage which applied in the Old Testament to Jehovah: "At the name of Jesus every knee should bow, in heaven and on earth and under the earth, and every tongue confess that Jesus Christ is Lord, to the glory of God the Father" (vv. 10, 11; cf. Isa. 45:23).

Peter, too, applied the term "God" to Christ, again in a passage which earlier translations have obscured. Second Peter 1:1, however, is correctly translated, "To those who through the righteousness of our God and Savior Jesus Christ have received a faith as precious as ours." We can see, therefore, that the New Testament showed Christ to be in truth God, on a level equal with the Father.

We turn, then, briefly to John's writings, and see their testimony. It need hardly be noted that the most obvious statement of the deity of Christ is John 1:1: "In the beginning was the Word, and the Word was with God, and the Word was God." The phrase θεὸς ἦν ὁ λόγος has been the object of innumerable studies, and it can confidently be said that it ascribes absolute deity to the Word. The translation "the Word was deity" is advocated by many scholars[5] and seems to be the best phrase to bring forth the meaning of the Greek. The predicate nominative, θεὸς, preceding the verb, is clearly qualitative (though in no sense can it be said to be indefinite), and hence bears the meaning of "that quality which to have is to be God," or simply "the state of being God." It is useless to attempt any other understanding of this phrase than that John intended for us to recognize that the Word himself is God.[6]

But the last phrase alone is not all that is important in this context. The whole passage, verses 1 to 3, spoke of the deity of the Logos, while at the same time showing within the deity, or within the nature of God, a distinction of persons: "In the beginning was the Word, and the Word was with God, and the Word was God. He was with God in the beginning. Through him all things were made; without him nothing was made that has been made." The two expressions "with God" (πρός τὸν θεόν) show the personal distinction within the Godhead. It is quite possible, in fact, that the one word πρός is here substituted for the common phrase πρόσωπον πρὸς πρόσωπον, "face to face," a phrase commonly used in Greek to show personal relationships.[7] The statements "in the beginning" (twice) and "through him all things were made" and "without him nothing was made that has been made" stress the eternity of the Word. He has existed for all time, he is the Creator of all things that have been made, and he himself therefore cannot be one of the created things (Paul made the same point in Colossians 1:15-18). Could it be possible to read this clause, being familiar with the opening verses of Genesis, and not think of the parallel?

We hardly need take note at this point of Christ's own declaration of his eternity in John 8:58, "Before Abraham was born, I am!" Yet this striking declaration deserves our attention. The response of the Jews shows that they knew precisely what was the implication of his statement. They attempted to stone him, the only possible charge being blasphemy, or as they put it in another instance, because he, being a man, made himself God (John 10:30-36). The claim to the divine name, and hence to the divine nature and eternity, is unmistakable in this passage.

In light of the passages above, only passing note is necessary with regard to Thomas' exclamation to Christ, "My Lord and my God" (John 20:28); Christ's statement, "I and the Father are one" (John 10:30); and John 5:18, where Christ was described as having claimed equality with God.

The testimony of the New Testament to the deity of Christ is unanimous. In the writings of Paul, he is "over all, God blessed forever." In John's writings he is "God," "equal with God," and "Alpha and Omega" (Rev. 22:7-16). In Peter's writings he is "our God and Savior Jesus Christ"; in James and Jude, which contain no explicit references to the deity of Christ, he is presented constantly on a parallel with "God" and with "the Father," and given equal glory and honor (James 1:1; 2:1; Jude 1, 4, 21, 25). In the Synoptics he is "the Son of God as well as the "Son of man"; God's kingdom is his (Matt. 12:28; 19:24; 21:31, 43; often in Mark and Luke); angels of God are his angels (Luke 12:8, 9; 15:10).

Were there no passages at all which directly call Christ God, we would still have a great weight of evidence that that is the New Testament conception of him, for in all senses he is depicted as precisely parallel to God the Father. C. F. D. Moule wrote:[8]

> Far more impressive than any single passage are two implicit Christological "pointers." The first is the fact that, in the greetings of the Pauline epistles, God and Christ are brought into a single formula. It requires an effort of imagination to grasp the enormity that this must have seemed to a non-Christian Jew. It must have administered a shock comparable (if the analogy may be allowed without irreverence) to our finding a religious Cu-

ban today inditing a message from God-and-"Che" Guevara. . . .

The other Christological pointer, evidenced early, because in the undeniably genuine Pauline epistles, is the fact that Paul seems to experience Christ as any theist reckons to understand God— that is, as personal, but as more than individual: as more than a person. This is evidenced by certain uses (though admittedly not all) of the well known incorporative formulae, "in Christ," "in the Lord," etc., and, to some extent, by the Pauline use of "the body," though this latter is mostly a metaphor for the organic harmony of a Christian congregation rather than a direct description of Christ as inclusive and incorporative. But, even on a minimal estimate, Paul's relation with Christ as thus described would be unthinkable, were Christ no more than a revered Rabbi, or a cult hero, or even a demigod.

In other words, throughout Paul's writings, Paul related to Christ as he related to God.

The conception of Christ's deity very often goes hand-in-hand with the conception of his eternity (John 1:1-3; Col. 1:15-18; Phil. 2:6-12; Rev. 22:7-16), and that is what we find in particular in Hebrews 1:3-12. In this passage the Son of God is not only "the exact representation of his being," but also is superior to the angels, being "begotten" of God, not created, and being worshiped by the angels. "Your throne, O God," the Father is represented as saying to the Son, "will last for ever and ever"; and "In the beginning, O Lord, you laid the foundations of the earth, and the heavens are the work of your hands. They will perish, but you remain; they will all wear out like a garment. You will roll them up like a robe; like a garment they will be changed. But you remain the same, and your years will never end." The eternal divine nature of Christ is spelled out clearly in such words, especially since they are presented as words of address from Father to Son. And this latter point, too, is important, for here again is an instance of a personal relation between the Father and the Son within the Godhead.

As surely as the New Testament teaches the deity of the Father, then, it teaches also the deity of the Son of God, Christ Jesus, the Word, the "only begotten God" (John 1:18). J. O. Buswell, Jr., argued[9] that μονογενής here and in John 3:16 is better represented by "unique" than by "only begotten."

THE HOLY SPIRIT IN
THE NEW TESTAMENT

When we come to the New Testament doctrine of the Holy Spirit, we enter an area in which controversy has raged throughout Church history. It has not been questioned so much whether the Spirit is presented as divine, or as God, as it has been questioned what the New Testament presents as the relation of the Holy Spirit to the Father and to the Son.

One theory often adopted is that the Holy Spirit is identified with the risen Christ (this was the position of Sabellius, a modalist of the third century, at whose teachings we will look more closely later). It has been taken up anew by the contemporary European theologian Dr. Hendrikus Berkhof.[10] This clearly is not the teaching of the New Testament. Moule wrote, "When one turns to the question of the Holy Spirit, one point that needs to be made at once is that it is by no means established that Paul ever identifies the Spirit with the risen Christ."[11] We can go a step further and say that it can be shown quite clearly that he distinguishes him from Christ.

The three texts most commonly taken to support

the view that identifies Christ with the Holy Spirit are
1 Corinthians 15:45: "the last Adam [became] a life-
giving spirit"; 2 Corinthians 3:17: "Now the Lord is
the Spirit . . ."; and Romans 8:9-11: where "Spirit of
Christ," "Spirit of God," "Christ," and "Spirit of him
who raised Jesus from the dead" are used, apparently
interchangeably.

The first text, despite some claims, does not support
this view. It is far more likely that it is a reference
simply to the deity of the Holy Spirit, for "the Spirit"
(τὸ πνεῦμα) is more likely the subject of the sentence,
and "the Lord" (ὁ κύριος) the predicate, than vice versa,
making the sentence read, ". . . the Spirit is the Lord."
With this construction, though it would still work with
the translation in the traditional order, it would be
natural to see a reference to the "Lord Jehovah" in
Exodus 34, the passage from which Paul was gleaning
this teaching. This is rather a text which actually
teaches the deity of the Holy Spirit. On the other hand,
many commentators, John Calvin included, take "the
Lord" here as referring to Christ, but identify "the
spirit" not with the Holy Spirit, but with "the spirit"
of the law, contrasted with "the letter" of the law, a
contrast made throughout the chapter. While either of
these interpretations would fit the context, to identify
the Holy Spirit with the risen Christ here would violate
both the context and the actual distinction between
Jesus and the Holy Spirit (1 Cor. 12:3-6; 2 Cor. 13:14).
Neither does the second text (1 Cor. 15:45), taken in
context, support the idea that the risen Christ is the
Holy Spirit in Paul's thought. Here Paul compared
Adam with Christ: "'The first man Adam became a
living being'; the last Adam, a life-giving spirit." In the
same context just referred to, Moule pointed out that
the comparison here is between ψυχή and πνεῦμα;
Adam became the former, while Christ "became" the
latter. It may be significant that Paul did not repeat

"became" (ἐγένετο), meaning that Paul simply considered Christ always a "life-giving spirit." Or, we may read it simply as an ellision on Paul's part, assuming it into the latter phrase. In Moule's words, Christ is "'spirit' and not merely a mortal self." It is true that the context speaks of Christ's resurrection, but there is nothing in it to suggest an identification here of Christ and the Holy Spirit, and the natural understanding is simply that in his Resurrection, the spiritual qualities in Christ rule over the physical, so that he has a "spiritual body" (v. 44), a body "sown in weakness, . . . raised in power; . . . sown a natural body, . . . raised a spiritual body."

The third text (Rom. 8:9-11) provides even less reason to think that Paul identified the Spirit with the risen Christ, for while it is predicated of both Christ and the Holy Spirit here that they dwell in the believer, there is no reason to think that this identifies them with each other. Correspondence of function cannot be made to imply identity of two objects, here any more than elsewhere. Romans 8:11, the last verse in the "prooftext," actually carries in it a clear distinction of Christ and the Holy Spirit: "And if the Spirit of him who raised Jesus from the dead is living in you, he who raised Christ from the dead will also give life to your mortal bodies through his Spirit, who lives in you." Again, while it is only by presupposition that one can force the interpretation of identity of Christ and the Holy Spirit on this passage, the context and the rest of Paul's usage show otherwise.

But if the Holy Spirit, in Paul's thought, is not to be identified with Christ, who is he? We have seen already that 2 Corinthians 3:17 very likely teaches the deity of the Holy Spirit by calling the Holy Spirit "the Lord," namely, in the context of the Lord of Exodus 34. The technique of applying Old Testament references to Jehovah to Christ and the Holy Spirit is familiar with

Paul. We noted above that he does it with Christ in Philippians 1:11, 12). Unfortunately, Paul seemed to assume the identity of the Holy Spirit, rather than belaboring the matter, which is to be expected. At that time groups were threatening early Christianity by questioning the identity of Christ, but apparently none were questioning the identity of the Spirit. Paul seemed to take the deity and distinct personality of the Spirit for granted.

Other texts also seem to show the deity of the Holy Spirit. Upon learning of the defrauding of the Church by Ananias and Sapphira, Peter said to Ananias, ". . . how is it that Satan has so filled your heart that you have lied to the Holy Spirit. . . . You have not lied to men but to God" (Acts 5:1-4). We have a double lesson here. First, the Holy Spirit is quite clearly seen as personal. The common antitrinitarian idea that the Holy Spirit is a mere force or energy by which God works, or indeed that the Spirit is simply the working of God, would make this passage senseless, for one cannot lie to an impersonal object or force. The passage shows also how clearly the early Church identified the Holy Spirit with God: to lie to the Holy Spirit is to lie to God.

There is further evidence in Acts 13:2. The Holy Spirit said: "Set apart for me Barnabas and Saul for the work to which I have called them." Not only is his personality evident here, but his deity as well, for he is the one who "called" Barnabas and Saul, and it is clear that he is the one who chose the work that they were to do. Paul, on the other hand, spoke in the opening verse of several of his epistles of the fact that he is an apostle "by the will of God." This text, of course, can be taken as no more than a pointer, and should not be pressed as a proof.

Granting, however, that the Holy Spirit is considered personal in the New Testament (see John 14:16, and the general teaching of Christ about the Spirit in John 14, 15, and 16), there is another text which is often neglected in studies of the deity of the Spirit. Hebrews 9:14 reads, ". . . much more, then, will the blood of Christ, who through the eternal Spirit offered himself unblemished to God, cleanse our consciences from acts that lead to death, so that we may serve the living God!" This speaks of an eternal personality, the Holy Spirit, and it is this eternal nature of the Holy Spirit which points out his deity. In the Old and New Testaments alike, God alone is truly eternal, and to speak of a person as eternal is to speak of that person as God.

This text brings us to an important point. If there were no explicit texts concerning the deity of Christ, and none at least strongly implying that of the Holy Spirit, it would be presumptuous to look to texts which present God (or "the Father"), Christ, and the Holy Spirit parallel to each other as though they were signs of a trinity. But granting at least that the New Testament clearly teaches the deity of Christ, and strongly implies the deity of the Holy Spirit, and presents Father, Son, and Spirit as distinct from each other (John 14:26, the Father sends the Spirit; 15:26, Jesus sends the Spirit; 17:8; 20:21, the Father sent Jesus), we may look at such passages in a new light, governed by these earlier findings. With such a background, texts which present the three as parallel to each other take on a strength which they would not have apart from that realization.

This is precisely what Hebrews 9:14 does. "Christ" presents himself "through the eternal Spirit" to "God," so that all three have a part in the work of redemption. The familiar usage of "God" to refer to the Father in distinction from the simple reference to deity was made by Paul in a similar context. "There are different kinds of gifts, but the same Spirit. There are different kinds of service, but the same Lord. There are different kinds of working, but the same God works all of them in all men" (1 Cor. 12:4-6). Whereas Hebrews refers to the work of redemption, Paul here refers to the post-redemptive work of God in Christians, equipping them for service to the Body of Christ, and in both passages the Father, Son, and Spirit are presented on a level parallel to each other. Paul used the same technique again: "May the grace of the Lord Jesus Christ, and the love of God, and the fellowship of the Holy Spirit be with you all" (2 Cor. 12:13). Taken apart from the strong indications of the deity of Christ and of the Spirit elsewhere, such texts would prove little, but with those texts in mind, these passages present a powerful view of the way in which the early Church looked on God (the Father), Christ, and the Holy Spirit as always working in perfect union, and related to all of them simply as they related to God.

There is much more which could be considered regarding the deity of the Holy Spirit. Christ's relation to him was certainly personal, and indeed we are shown that Christ related to him during his ministry in a role of dependence (Matt. 4:1; Luke 4:1), a relation quite similar to that displayed toward his Father (John 5:19). Also, it is by the anointing of the Spirit that Jesus was prepared for ministry (Luke 4:18, 19), and it is often reiterated that Jesus went about "in the power of the Spirit" (Luke 5:14). There is then in the life of the incarnate Word of God a relation to the Father and to the Holy Spirit which can only be seen as cooperation and equality of nature.

It is this relation of Christ to the Father and the Spirit which Dr. John A. T. Robinson takes as one of the strongest indications of triunity in the Godhead:

> At the Incarnation . . . the Godhead is revealed for the first time as existing in three distinct *relations*. It is these differences of relation that make necessary a doctrine of the Trinity, not differences of

"character" or modes of working. The Old Testament, too, knew God in different "characters," but it was not forced to a Trinitarian Theology. . . . We cannot begin with God creating, God redeeming, God sanctifying, or any other such collection of attributes, and then proceed to identify these with Father, Son, and Holy Spirit. . . . Rather, one must start with the three Persons, no more and no less, which are required by the three relations at the Incarnation.[12]

The New Testament presents a consistent picture of three distinct persons, Father, Son, and Holy Spirit, all of whom are assigned status as deity, who relate to each other on a coordinate level, who share in the works of creation, redemption, and sanctification, and who in every way are related to by New Testament believers, each in turn and all in unison, as God. Yet they are consistently presented not as three Gods but as one. And this, after all, is what it is to teach the doctrine of the Trinity as conceived at Nicea, if not in such precise terms, at least with substantially the same meaning.

When we have said these three things, then—that there is but one God, that the Father and the Son and the Spirit is each God, that the Father and the Son and the Spirit is each a distinct person—we have enunciated the doctrine of the Trinity in its completeness.[13]

While we have been able to arrive fairly quickly at a New Testament doctrine of the Trinity, it did not come so easily for the early Church. A triune conception of God existed from the earliest times in the Church (we have already seen it in the New Testament), a conception in which Father, Son, and Spirit were related to as one God. But the careful formulation of this conception drawn from experience and from the teachings of Jesus and the apostles into words which could resist misinterpretation took the hard work of three centuries after the death of the last of the apostles. Such work took place in the atmosphere of constant debate, controversy, and resistance of misinterpretation and misapplication. It is to this development which we now turn.

II

THE DOCTRINE OF THE TRINITY IN THE ANTE-NICENE FATHERS

IN examining the doctrine of the Trinity, one needs to go back to a time before the so-called "Ante-Nicene Fathers," to one of the earliest of Christian documents, the *Didache*, for what may be an early reference to trinitarianism.

THE DOCTRINE OF THE TRINITY IN THE FIRST CENTURY

Records of first-century Christian teaching are limited to the New Testament, the *Didache*, the writings of Clement of Rome (A.D. 70?), Barnabas (A.D. 75?), and Hermas (A.D. 78-85?),[1] aside from some fragments, pseudepigraphic materials, and gnostic writings.

In the first chapter we said that the New Testament presents a view in which three persons, the Father, the Son, and the Holy Spirit, are conceived to be the same God, though still distinct from each other. This conception resulted in applying parallel constructions to the three (1 Cor. 12:4-6; 2 Cor. 13:14; Heb. 9:14). The most famous of these constructions is the command of Jesus: "Therefore go and make disciples of all nations, baptizing them in the name of the Father and of the Son and of the Holy Spirit" (Matt. 28:19). Here is precisely the sort of construction we saw in Paul and the writer to the Hebrews, yet much more explicit. Believers are to be baptized into "the name" of "the Father and of the Son and of the Holy Spirit."

This text is attacked by many higher critics. Yet the authenticity of the text is supported by the strongest manuscript evidence. That it was in the earliest manuscripts of this Gospel must now be admitted by all. Nevertheless it is impugned as impossible of Jesus' lips: the objection, it seems, stems not from an objective comparison of this with the rest of Jesus' teaching in the Synoptics and John's Gospel as from a presupposition that Jesus himself did not teach such "high" theology. This seems entirely contrary to the evidence of the documents themselves. All four Gospels present Jesus to be as much God as he is man. They use the titles "Son of Man" and "Son of God," show him speaking of God as his own Father in a special sense not true of any others, communing with the Father and the Spirit in the most intimate way—again impossible for any but himself. And they show him generally conscious of his divine authority as the King of the Kingdom of God both now and in the future.

The phrase, "in the name of the Father and of the Son and of the Holy Spirit" would take on a very important meaning for early Christians since it was quite probably the formula used at baptism in the early Church. Christian instruction prior to baptism would thus include discussion of the meaning of the formula. With the rest of the New Testament teaching on the Godhead in the background, it seems impossible that the early Church did not have a triune concept of the Deity, even if it did not have precise formulae for expressing such a concept. It must be remembered that precision of statement is not necessary for accuracy of belief or experience, and that such precision comes not so much from casual thinking on a subject as from defending one's concept and keeping it from being misinterpreted. There is nothing to make us think that the early Church's triune conception of God was attacked or misinterpreted. In other words, the fact that in the earliest times of the Church there is little explicit or precise statement, and even less definition of the doctrine of the Trinity, does not mean that the Church did not believe it. It could mean that misinterpretations and attacks against it were few.

Outside the New Testament, the chief first-century trinitarian reference appears in the *Didache* (A.D. 35-60), in another reference to baptism.

> But concerning baptism, thus shall ye baptize. Having first recited all these things, baptize *in the name of the Father and of the Son and of the Holy Spirit* in living (running) water. . . . But if thou hast neither, then pour water on the head thrice in the name of the Father and of the Son and of the Holy Spirit.[2]

If we are correct above in thinking that an initiatory rite, especially that of baptism, which uses the phrase "in the name" will carry with it a substantial package of teaching, then we may assume that here again we have an intimation of trinitarian belief in the first century.

THE DOCTRINE OF THE TRINITY IN THE SECOND CENTURY

In the second century trinitarian thought becomes more pronounced. The emphasis in this century, as in the third and fourth, is far more on the deity of Christ than of the Holy Spirit (again because this was the controversial point), but as in the first century, the primary thought was of monotheism, the basis of Judeo-Christian theology:

> The doctrine of one God, the Father and creator, formed the background and indisputable premise of the Church's faith. Inherited from Judaism, it was her bulwark against pagan polytheism, Gnostic emanationism and Marcionite dualism. The problem for theology was to integrate with it, intellectually, the fresh data of the specifically Christian revelation. Reduced to their simplest, these were the convictions that God had made Himself known in the Person of Jesus, the Messiah, raising Him from the dead and offering salvation through Him, and that He had poured out His Holy Spirit upon the Church.[3]

The eternity of the Person of Christ was one of the beliefs which was the most carefully defended. It was popular among some people to say that Jesus did not actually exist prior to the Incarnation. Ignatius, writing around A.D. 110-120 (possibly, but not likely, as late as 130-140), answered this by pointing out the distinction between the Divine and human natures of Christ:

> We have also as a Physician the Lord our God, Jesus the Christ, the only-begotten Son and Word, before time began, but who afterwards became also man, of Mary the virgin. For "the Word was made flesh." Being incorporeal, He was in the body; being impassible, He was in a passible body; being immortal, He was in a mortal body; being life, He became subject to corruption, that He might free our souls from death and corruption,

and heal them, and might restore them to health, when they were diseased with ungodliness and wicked lusts.[4]

Ignatius here teaches clearly that Christ is "the Lord our God," and sets his generation as "before time began," that is, in eternity. He also takes up a theme which is repeated again and again throughout the literature of the Church Fathers and in the New Testament as well: the Deity and the humanity of Christ are both intimately related to his work as Redeemer. "The Lord our God" became man "that He might free our souls." In the New Testament we find the same teaching (Heb. 2:5-17; 9:14), the idea being that he only can mediate properly between God and man who is equal with both parties (1 Tim. 2:5). We will see this theme again especially in the fourth-century apologist against the Arians, Athanasius.

Another of the Apologists of the second century, Justin Martyr (A.D. 114-162-168), brings back the familiar triune formula for the baptismal rite:

> For, in the name of God, the Father and Lord of the universe, and of our Saviour Jesus Christ, and of the Holy Spirit, they then receive the washing with water (*First Apol.*, LXI).[5]

A contemporary of Justin, the Church historian Irenaeus (ca. A.D. 115-190), a disciple of Polycarp, who was in turn a disciple of the Apostle John, developed trinitarian statements further. In his *Against Heresies* X.1, he wrote:

> The Church, though dispersed throughout the whole world, even to the ends of the earth, has received from the apostles and their disciples this faith: [She believes] in one God, the Father Al-

mighty, Maker of heaven, and earth, and the sea, and all things that are in them; and in one Christ Jesus, the Son of God, who became incarnate for our salvation; and in the Holy Spirit, who proclaimed through the prophets the dispensations of God, and the advents, and the birth from a virgin, and the passion, and the resurrection from the dead, and the ascension into heaven in the flesh of the beloved Christ Jesus, our Lord, and His [future] manifestation from heaven in the glory of the Father "to gather all things in one," and to raise up anew all flesh of the whole human race, in order that to Christ Jesus, our Lord, and God, and Saviour, and King, according to the will of the invisible Father, "every knee should bow, of things in heaven, and things in earth, and things under the earth, and that every tongue should confess" to Him, and that He should execute just judgment towards all. . . .[6]

In another of his writings he stated the doctrine even more strongly:

This, then, is the order of the rule of our faith. . . . God the Father, not made, not material, invisible; one God, the creator of all things: this is the first point of our faith. The second point is this: the Word of God, Son of God, Christ Jesus our Lord, Who was manifested to the prophets according to the form of their prophesying and according to the method of the Father's dispensation; through Whom (i.e. the Word) all things were made; Who also, at the end of the age, to complete and gather up all things, was made man among men, visible and tangible, in order to abolish death and show forth life and produce perfect reconciliation be-

50

THE TRINITY IN THE ANTE-NICENE FATHERS

tween God and man. And the third point is: the
Holy Spirit, through Whom the prophets prophe-
sied, and the Fathers learned the things of God,
and the righteous were led into the way of righteousness; Who at the end of the age was poured
out in a new way upon mankind in all the earth,
renewing man to God.[7]

Here, less than a century after the death of the last
apostle, the faith has begun to be stated in a formalized
pattern. We must constantly remind ourselves how
short a time after the apostolic period the second century—beginning to end—really is. If Irenaeus did live
until A.D. 190, as seems to be the case, then he brings
the second generation after John to the very end of the
second century, and overlaps the life of Tertullian for
forty-five years and Hippolytus for twenty. The close-
ness of the relation of these writers to the apostolic age
cannot be underestimated, for the powerful shaping
force of those first followers of Jesus would surely continue even by purely oral tradition, let alone the powerful control their writings had, for at least three generations of Christians. It is wrong to say that the
Trinity is far separated from apostolic teaching, even
if we neglect the fact that it is taught in the New
Testament, for the apostles' hold over the first several
generations of Christians connects them strongly with
what those later Christians taught.

In the second statement quoted from Irenaeus above,
he reiterated the connection of the divinity of Christ
with his work in saving man: it is only as deity that
Christ has the authority to take away sin; but on the
other hand, it is only as humanity that Christ can be
the representative of mankind to pay for sin.

Another second-century thinker, Athenagoras, ap-
proached Christology from the philosophical point of

view. The dates of his birth and death are completely unknown, but internal evidences lead to the conclusion that his writings were penned between A.D. 170 and 180. According to early tradition, "he was occupied with searching the Scriptures for arguments against Christianity, when he was suddenly converted."[8] His conceptions are at least to some extent neo-Platonic, but the influence of the Old and New Testaments can be seen clearly in his writings.

Athenagoras' theology is primarily that of the Logos. He was concerned with identifying who the Logos was and what his relation was to God the Father. His conclusion was that the Logos is the Son of God, who became incarnate as the man Christ Jesus, and one with the Father:

> That we are not atheists, therefore, seeing that we acknowledge one God, uncreated, eternal, invisible, impassible, incomprehensible, illimitable, who is apprehended by the understanding only and the reason, who is encompassed by light, and beauty, and spirit, and power ineffable, by whom the universe has been created through His Logos, and set in order, and is kept in being—I have sufficiently demonstrated. [I say "His Logos"], for we acknowledge also a Son of God. Nor let any one think it ridiculous that God should have a Son. For though the poets, in their fictions, represent the gods as no better than men, our mode of thinking is not the same as theirs, concerning either God the Father or the Son. But the Son of God is the Logos of the Father, in idea and in operation; for after the pattern of Him and by Him were all things made, the Father and the Son being one. And, the Son being in the Father and the Father in the Son, in oneness and power of spirit, the

52

understanding and reason (νοῦς καὶ λόγος) of the Father is the Son of God.[9]

Athenagoras' Christology actually brings us surprisingly close to the Christological formulations of the fourth century, though he predates them by over 130 years. We find here the doctrines of the eternity of the Logos, the coinherence of the Father and the Son (although this should be no surprise, since it is Jesus' teaching also; John 14:1-10), the union of the Father and Son (again based on Christ's teaching; John 10:30), and the work of the Logos in creation (John 1:1-3).

But Athenagoras does not rest with Christology. He has a well-developed doctrine of the Holy Spirit as well. As in the New Testament, the Holy Spirit is presented on a level with the Father and the Son, involved in their workings in the divine οἰκονομία (plan, or dispensation):

> The Holy Spirit Himself also, which operates in the prophets, we assert to be an effluence of God, flowing from Him, and returning back again like a beam of the sun. Who, then would not be astonished to hear men who speak of God the Father, and of God the Son, and of the Holy Spirit, and who declare both their power in union and their distinction in order, called atheists?[10]

Perhaps the most famous trinitarian reference from the second century is the statement of Theophilus (116–181), another writer who is only shortly removed from the last of the apostles. His is the first use of the word "Trinity" in Christian literature which is extant:

> In like manner also the three days which were before the luminaries, are types of the Trinity, of God, and His Word, and His wisdom.[11]

It is instructive to note that this use of τρίαδ (here in the genitive, τριάδος) is singularly unassuming. The use of the word here bears all the marks of a word which had long before become a commonplace in the Christian community. One does not speak obliquely of "types" of something with which one's readers are not at least fairly well acquainted. So while we may date this use of the word sometime from, broadly speaking, A.D. 150-175, we are forced to assume that the word was in regular use before that. It would not be unreasonable to guess that it has roots as early as three to five decades before, perhaps even earlier. This brings us back again to the early part of the second century. And even this, the earliest *known* use of the word, remains within two generations of the last of the apostles.

The concept of Trinity in unity, three distinct persons who are the one God, is then firmly entrenched in Christian thought by the middle to late second century, and has even acquired a special term to refer to it: τρίαδ. It remains in accord, in substance, with the teaching of the New Testament; and despite the fact that this new term has been applied to it, the vocabulary of trinitarian thought remains that of the New Testament: the Father and Son are "one," the Father is in the Son and the Son in the Father, and the Holy Spirit is one with them. It was in the third century that more sophisticated development occurred, as trinitarian thought confronted attacks and misinterpretations which forced its adherents to define precisely what it was that they believed.

THE DOCTRINE OF THE TRINITY IN THE THIRD CENTURY

History does not fit neatly into hundred-year packages. The worlds of politics, philosophy, and the arts do not close shop at the end of the ninety-ninth year of a century, and open the curtains anew on the following. The same holds true for the history of Christianity. We saw that the ideas of the thinkers of the second century evolved directly from those of the first, and now we will see that the ideas, and the lives also, of the third-century Christian leaders spring out of the second.

We noted that Irenaeus probably lived to A.D. 190, and that he was the contemporary of Tertullian for about forty-five years, and Hippolytus for about twenty. The influence of this man second in succession from John is still strong when we enter the third century.

Tertullian was born about A.D. 145 and did the major part of his writing from about 190-200. Nevertheless, it seems almost necessary to place him among third-century Christians (he died between about 220 and 240). He was converted around 185, and became a presbyter in Carthage in 190, taking his place among the leaders of Christianity in his locale. He is often termed the "founder" of Latin theology. His ideas were far advanced over most of those of the second century, and the milieu in which he lived his Christian life is far different. Monasticism was gaining strength, Christianity had weathered the worst of her persecutions from Rome, and a great many schisms were beginning to test the strength of the faith. Tertullian himself fell prey, sometime after 200, to one of them, the Montanists. The Montanists emphasized the contemporary role of the Holy Spirit in prophecy in the Church, but did not, apparently, deny the doctrine of the Trinity. Fairly distinct lines were already apparent between "orthodoxy" and "heresy." The test of orthodoxy was agreement with the teachings handed down, in writing or in word, from the apostles, and with the teachings of the Old Testament and the apostolic writings. Though the canonization of the New Testament had not occurred in a complete or systematic way, still most, if not all, of the books of the New Testament are quoted or referred to by writers prior to this time, and always given the place of highest authority. By then the Church had begun to think of herself as "catholic," a term which at first expressed her universality, and later came to have the added connotation of orthodoxy.

Tertullian's formulations of the doctrine of the Trinity are quite sophisticated, and clearly foreshadow the formulation decided upon at the Council of Nicea. "The Latin word for Trinity (*trinitas*), occurs for the first time in Tertullian's [*Against Praxeas*], and his phrases *tres personae* and *una substantia* anticipated the orthodox trinitarian formula." A. C. McGiffert described in further depth Tertullian's concept of the Trinity:

> [Tertullian's] idea of God well illustrates his general attitude. In his tract against Praxeas, the most theological of his writings, he formulated over against Praxeas' monarchianism a doctrine of the Trinity essentially legal in character. That God is triune means primarily that he is three persons in the legal sense, that is, three persons who share or own in common one substance or property. Tertullian's language at this point, though not the legal interpretation that attached to it, later had influence in east as well as west.[12]

Tertullian's primary theological writing was done in response to the heresy of Monarchianism, which so stressed the unity of the Godhead that it destroyed the concept of plurality. Thus, while on the one hand, Tertullian, too, believed firmly that God is one, he needed to stress in opposition to Monarchianism the plurality involved in the Godhead. He wrote in terms which we could expect to see in the fourth century as easily as the third:

> Thus the connection of the Father in the Son, and of the Son in the Paraclete, produces three coherent Persons, *who are yet distinct* One from Another. These Three are one *essence*, not one *Person*, as it is said, "I and my Father are One," in respect of unity of substance, not singularity of number.[13]

Here Tertullian was writing in response to one of the favorite prooftexts of the Monarchians who believed that Jesus was the Father, and that therefore the Father himself was born, suffered, and died. In John 10:30, Jesus said, "I and the Father are one," a text this group never tired of quoting. However, Tertullian saw a fine point in what Jesus had said: The word for *one* is neuter (Gr. ἐν; Lat. *unum*), not masculine, meaning that their unity is one of substance, not of person. As Kelly puts it:[14]

> . . . the Saviour's claim, "I and my Father are one" (*unum*), indicates that the Three are "one reality" (*unum* is neuter), not "one Person" (*unus*), pointing as it does to identity of substance and not mere numerical unity.

It is this balance of substantial unity and personal plurality which Tertullian so emphasized throughout his discussions of the Trinity (Roberts and Donaldson, *Ante-Nicene Fathers*, Vol. 3, p. 598, *Against Praxeas*, ii.). He responded to a Monarchian argument by writing:

> As if in this way also one were not All, in that All are of One, by unity (that is) of substance; while

the mystery of the dispensation is still guarded, which distributes the Unity into a Trinity, placing in their order the three *Persons*—the Father, the Son, and the Holy Ghost; three, however, not in condition (Lat. *statu*), but in degree; not in substance, but in form; not in power, but in aspect; yet of one substance, and of one condition, and of one power, inasmuch as He is one God, from whom these degrees and forms and aspects are reckoned, under the name of the Father, and of the Son, and of the Holy Ghost.

The unity of substance of Father and Son (and of Spirit also) is a unity in plurality, the plurality being seen in the relation of the persons to one another.

The thought here is of two persons sharing equally in a single substance, so that each is fully God, lacking nothing of the substance of deity. In other contexts Tertullian extended this concept to the Holy Spirit as well, rounding out the Trinity. He wrote in his *Apology*, ". . . so, too, that which has come forth out of God is at once God and the Son of God, and the two are one. In this way also, as He is Spirit of Spirit and God of God, He is made a second in manner of existence— in position, not in nature; and He did not withdraw from the original source, but went forth."[15]

It has been thought that Tertullian's concept could fit the idea of polytheism by saying that the unity of substance is simply a generic, not a numeric, unity. This, in fact, was the accusation of the Monarchians, and it was their overwhelming desire to avoid polytheism which led them to the error of denying the distinction of persons in the Trinity. However, there can be no real misunderstanding of Tertullian when his views are read in context. Not only does he speak of three persons and one substance, he also makes it very clear that these three persons and one substance are all the same one and only God:

> We, however, as we indeed always have done ... believe that there is only one God, but under the following dispensation, or οἰκονομία, as it is called, that this one only God has also a Son, His Word, who proceeded from Himself, by whom all things were made, and without whom nothing was made. Him we believe to have been sent by the Father into the Virgin, and to have been born of her—being both Man and God, the Son of Man and the Son of God, and to have been called by the name of Jesus Christ; we believe Him to have suffered, died, and been buried, according to the Scriptures, and, after He had been raised again by the Father and taken back to heaven, to be sitting at the right hand of the Father, and that He will come to judge the quick and the dead; who sent also from heaven from the Father, according to His own promise, the Holy Ghost, the Paraclete, the sanctifier of the faith of those who believe in the Father, and in the Son, and in the Holy Ghost.[16]

The next great defender of trinitarian faith was Hippolytus. Like Tertullian, his primary writing was apologetic, and also like Tertullian, his concentration was in refuting Monarchian heresies regarding the Trinity. While he had much to say about Praxeas, Tertullian's archenemy in the faith, he concentrated more on successive modalism, which held that the Father became the Son. In its more developed forms the theory went on to say that the Son became the Holy Spirit, one person emanating out from himself, remaining only a single person, but taking up different roles or "modes" (hence the term "modalism" for this heresy) in relation to creation.

Hippolytus, born in A.D. 170, was a disciple of Irenaeus. He took many of his ideas from Irenaeus, and developed his doctrine of the Trinity along those lines. We are not surprised, then, to see him develop a concept which strongly emphasized the unity of the three persons as one God, for Irenaeus, in resisting paganism, found it necessary to reiterate the Christian belief in monotheism many times. But at the same time, Hippolytus had to battle the extremist thinking of the Monarchians, who took monotheism as the only basic principle, and failed to recognize the plurality of persons in the one God.

Hippolytus, with Tertullian, recognized that this modalistic concept of the Trinity would destroy the sense of the inner relations of the Father, Son, and Spirit which they found so pronounced in the New Testament, and the different relations which they themselves experienced with Father, Son, and Spirit in their Christian lives. He also recognized the dangerous implications of the modalistic idea which allowed for the assumption of such different forms by the one God. It could, and in some thinkers did, lead to an emanationalism akin to gnostic monism, in which the distinction between God as Creator and everything else as creature is nullified. He stressed the Creator/creature distinction when he wrote:

> The Logos alone of this God is from God himself;
> wherefore also the *Logos* is God, being *the* substance of God. Now the world was made from nothing; wherefore *it* is not God. . . .[17]

Hippolytus' teaching on the Trinity was not so much positive, as was Tertullian's, as negative, in that he erected bulwarks against misinterpretation. For those who would accuse trinitarianism of being polytheistic, he responded that the Logos, as the one who is truly "from God himself," is the very substance of God himself, and hence is no other God. To those, on the other hand, who would respond to this by saying that, if that is the case, then the Son must be the Father generated, he responded that the Father and Son are distinct persons, even though they are the same substance.

The primary schismatic sects of the third century had little to say about the Holy Spirit. They were more interested in the identity of the Father and the Son. So, it was on this subject that the Fathers of the third century had to concentrate as well. While in Novatian of Rome we have a full-fledged doctrine of the Trinity (he wrote a complete treatise on the subject). He spent most of his time however primarily defending the unity of substance of the Father and the Son as the one God, while acknowledging their personal distinction from each other. He reasoned that Father and Son must be the same God, for only God is eternal, yet if the Father is God, he is eternally Father, therefore the Son must be eternal also. His dependence on New Testament writings is evidenced constantly in his own words: "But this Word whereby all things were made [is God]. 'And God,' says he, 'was the Word.' Therefore God proceeded from God, in that the Word which proceeded is God, who proceeded forth from God."[18] He saw the Deity of the Son taught as clearly in the New Testament as his humanity:

> For Scripture as much announces Christ as also God, as it announces God Himself as man. It has as much described Jesus Christ to be man, as moreover it has also described Christ the Lord to be God. Because it does not set forth Him to be the

Son of God only, but also the Son of man; nor does it only say, the Son of man, but it has also been accustomed to speak of Him as the Son of God. So that being of both, He is both, lest if He should be one only, He could not be the other. For as nature itself has prescribed that he must be believed to be a man who is of man, so the same nature prescribes also that He must be believed to be God who is of God; but if he should not also be God when he is of God, no more should he be man although he should be of man. And thus both doctrines would be endangered in one and the other way, by one being convicted to have lost belief in the other. Let them, therefore, who read that Jesus Christ the Son of man is man, read also that this same Jesus is called also God and the Son of God.[19]

The next great thinker of the third century was Origen. In sheer volume his writings outweigh many of the other Church Fathers put together. A prolific philosophical theologian, Origen turned the full force of his powerful mind against Monarchianism in his jealousy for the personal distinctions in the Godhead. There is a curious problem in Origen's writings, however, in that he becomes quite inconsistent. Philip Schaff writes:

Origen, on the one hand, attributed to Christ eternity and other divine attributes which logically lead to the orthodox doctrine of the identity of substance; so that he was vindicated even by Athanasius, the two Cappadocian Gregories, and Basil. But, on the other hand, in his zeal for the personal distinctions in the Godhead he taught with equal clearness a separateness of essence between the Father and the Son, and the subordination of the Son, as a second or secondary God beneath the Father, and thus furnished a starting point for the Arian heresy.[20]

Origen did teach that Christ was both God and man:

In the first place, we must note that the nature of that deity which is in Christ in respect of His being the only-begotten Son of God is one thing, and that human nature which He assumed in these last times for the purposes of the dispensation (of grace) is another.[21]

Origen may have considered the divine nature something which could subsist not only in distinct Persons, as the orthodox doctrine of the Trinity taught, but in separate beings. He took the substantial unity of Father and Son as a generic, and not a numerical unity. This teaching opened the way for Arianism to teach its doctrine of the Son as a lesser God, though of course Arianism went further than Origen and denied that the Son shares the same nature as the Father. Arianism took Origen's subordinationism with his apparently generic concept of the nature of God, added its denial of the eternity of the Logos, and arrived at polytheism.

The keystone of Origen's teaching was the eternal generation of the Logos. In one passage he both defined what he thought it meant for something to be "eternal," and attributed precisely this to the "wisdom" of God, the Son, the Logos:

That is properly termed everlasting or eternal which neither had a beginning of existence, nor can ever cease to be what it is. And this is the idea conveyed by John when he says that "God is light." Now His wisdom is the splendour of that light, not only in respect of its being light, but also of being everlasting light, so that His wisdom is eternal and everlasting splendour. If this be fully understood, it clearly shows that the existence of the Son is derived from the Father, but not in time, nor from any other beginning, except, as we have said, from God Himself.[22]

Origen also has a definite doctrine of the Holy Spirit as a member of the Godhead. He, with the Father and the Son, is eternal.

For if [the Holy Spirit were not eternally as He is, and had received knowledge at some time and then became the Holy Spirit] this were the case, the Holy Spirit would never be reckoned in the Unity of the Trinity, i.e., along with the unchangeable Father and His Son, unless He had always been the Holy Spirit. When we use, indeed, such terms as "always," or "was," or any other designation of time, they are not to be taken absolutely, but with due allowance; for while the significations of these words relate to time, and those subjects of which we speak are spoken of by a stretch of language as existing in time, they nevertheless surpass in their real nature all conception of the finite understanding. [23]

Not only, however, are the Son and the Holy Spirit both said by Origen to be eternal. They are both said to be of the very same nature of deity of which the Father is: "For it is one and the same thing to have a share in the Holy Spirit, which is [the Spirit] of the Father and the Son, since the nature of the Trinity is one and incorporeal." The oneness of the nature of the Trinity here taught would seem to militate against Origen's subordinationism; but apparently he was not aware of the inconsistencies in his doctrine which later proved fertile ground for the growth of Arianism.

In Tertullian, Hippolytus, and Novatian we meet a clarity on the doctrine of the Trinity which is clearly lacking in the thought of Origen. Nevertheless, he takes his place with those three as one of the leading thinkers of the third century; and indeed, the acuteness of his philosophical insight probably exceeds theirs in all areas except that of the balancing of the distinction of persons with the unity of nature. While Origen turned constantly to Scripture, it was always with allegorical interpretations which allowed his neoplatonic philosophy, rather than the Scriptures, to govern his theology, and through that, his philosophy.

There were, of course, other thinkers during the first three centuries of the Christian Church, many of whom had something to say about the doctrine of the Trinity. In the men we have observed, however, we find the height of Christian trinitarianism prior to the Council of Nicea. When we reach Origen and Novatian (the latter lived to about A.D. 280, the former only until ca. 254), having already seen the teaching of Tertullian and Hippolytus, we have seen the doctrine taken as far as it will go until the fourth century, and particularly the Council of Nicea (A.D. 325).

Up to this time, excluding the inconsistencies of Origen, the orthodox doctrine of the Trinity remains in substance precisely what we found in the New Testament. Some new terminology entered the discussion: words such as "Trinity," ὑπόστασις, and οὐσία in Greek, and *persona* and *substantia* in Latin; but the vocabulary was used to express the same thoughts. This pattern continued throughout the fourth century.

At this point, it is necessary to become familiar with some of the heresies which form the background to fourth-century controversies. Just as heterodox conceptions spurred orthodox Christian thinkers into action in formulating, defining, and defending the doctrine of the Trinity in the first three centuries, so they did in the fourth century also; and the unorthodox views which spurred apologetics were apparent by the end of the third century.

UNORTHODOX CONCEPTS OF THE TRINITY BEFORE A.D. 300

The development of the doctrine of the Trinity must be seen in perspective with the many unorthodox attempts to define it. We must realize that, in essence, all of the conceptions of the doctrine attempted the same task: to devise a consistent means of combining a commitment to monotheism and the authority of the Old Testament. Some also recognized the authority of the apostolic writings and other writings now in the New Testament canon. They held to the conviction that God had shown himself to men in Jesus Christ, and had made himself available to men in some way in the Holy Spirit.

The word "orthodox" comes from the Greek ὀρθός and δοκεῖν, "straight" and "to appear." Its primary meaning is simply "that which looks straight," or "that which looks right." In the early Church the criteria for "appearing straight" were two: adherence to what they believed to be divinely inspired teaching, including the Old Testament and the teachings of the apostles; and logical consistency. The authority of the apostles was considered to be attached to the writings of the immediate companions of the apostles; in some instances, with Luke as the companion of Paul, and Mark as the companion of Peter.

The first system of thought with which we have to deal is gnosticism, a highly syncretistic system of thought which ranged over the sects of both Christianity and the lingering Greek pagan religions, Babylonian mysteries, and perhaps the Egyptian mystery cults. Its forms were numerous, and perhaps should not be referred to as a single system at all. Gnosticism had a way of assimilating into its thought the concepts taught by religions with which it came into contact.

The chief focus of gnosticism was on γνῶσις, "knowledge." The object of the Gnostics was to acquire a special, deeply hidden knowledge about the cosmos not available to the ordinary man. There was no single source of authority in this knowledge, and perhaps one of the great weaknesses of the movement was that it had no definite criteria for discerning the truth or falsehood of religious (or even secular) ideas. Its speculations on cosmology as a result became wild and uncontrolled, producing some of the strangest, most interesting systems in the history of philosophy and religion. It would not be wrong to say that it sometimes, if not often, mistook "interesting" for "true."

There were two main strains of gnosticism: metaphysical monism, and metaphysical dualism. The former believed all reality to be one; and as part of this system there arose theories of the emanation of the cosmos out of the divine monad, proposing different levels of reality, while in fact all reality was one. Metaphysical dualism was the opposite—a system in which a strict distinction between the creator and the creature was to be maintained at all costs. This meant that the creator could not come in contact with created things, for this would introduce impurities into his nature. The question naturally arose of how creation had come about, if the creator could not come into contact with it. Two answers were given: (1) Some taught that creation itself was eternal, just as was the creator, and thus they took metaphysical dualism to its absolute extreme. (2) Others decided that when the creator took it in mind to create, he first emanated out of himself a Logos, or reason, which had in it all the principles and designs of the intended creation. This effulgence did the actual task of creating and ordering the material universe.

The two types of cosmology resulted in two types of ethics, both of which, however, had the same foundation: ethical dualism. Metaphysical dualism saw an absolute ethical antithesis between God and the creation, and hence believed that the creation itself must be evil. Metaphysical monism, on the other hand, saw all reality as varying forms of God, but believed that the purest form of God was absolute monad; so it, too, conceived all divisible, corporeal things as evil in relation to the monad.

Ethical dualism, in turn, brought two opposite results. First, it encouraged asceticism, a harsh restraint from all physical desires, a denial of the flesh (since it was considered evil). But second, it brought antinomianism, a complete disregard for all ethical imperatives and rules. If, with metaphysical dualism, one believes all matter is totally evil, why bother with it? And if, with metaphysical monism, all matter is really only another form of God, the lowest type of reality, then it is in a sense not real at all; and again, why bother with it?

The gnostic conception of the Trinity was essentially emanational; that is, it conceived of the Son of God as the emanation from the creator, the divine monad, which was the first form of reality down from the purest form, absolute one. There does not appear to have been much speculation about the nature of the Holy Spirit in gnosticism, but in general he was conceived to be yet another emanation, this time from the Logos. Thus gnosticism had a hierarchical, subordinationist conception of the Triad, a conception which greatly affected Origen's thought and the thought of the ομοιούσιαν party of the fourth century. There was, then, no real conception here of three persons sharing equally in the single substance of deity.

Gnosticism and Monarchianism in all their forms were condemned by the general Christian conscience and were battled in the writings of Tertullian, Hippolytus, Novatian, Origen, and Dionysius of Alexandria, among others, in the third century. The condemnation of these systems was repeated by all the Fathers of the fourth century who subscribed to the Nicene idea of the Trinity. In Origen, however, we approach a subject deeply entangled in inconsistencies and interpretational difficulty.

Many Christian scholars have pointed out the subordinationism in Origen's teaching on the Trinity. The noted historian of doctrine, J. N. D. Kelly, wrote that subordinationism in Origen's thinking was "epitomized in the statement that, whereas the Father's action extends to all reality, the Son's is limited to rational beings, and the Spirit's to those who are being sanctified."[24] The statement to which he referred reads as follows:

> Having made these declarations regarding the Unity of the Father, and of the Son, and of the Holy Spirit, let us return to the order in which we began the discussion. God the Father bestows upon all, existence; and participation in Christ, in respect of His being the word of reason, renders them rational beings. From which it follows that they are deserving either of praise or blame, because capable of virtue and vice. On this account, therefore, is the grace of the Holy Ghost present, that those beings which are not holy in their essence may be rendered holy by participating in it. Seeing, then, that firstly, they derive their existence from

God the Father; secondly, their rational nature from the Word; thirdly, their holiness from the Holy Spirit. . .those who have been previously sanctified by the Holy Spirit are again made capable of receiving Christ, in respect that He is the righteousness of God; and those who have earned advancement to this grade by the sanctification of the Holy Spirit, will nevertheless obtain the gift of wisdom according to the power and working of the Spirit of God.

Taken by itself, this could easily be given a subordinationist meaning. We must remember, however, that there are portions of the teaching of Jesus which can be treated this way. In John 14:28 he declared that the Father is greater than he. But taken in context, we should not interpret Jesus' statement in that manner, for earlier in the same chapter he taught the complete coinherence of himself with the Father, and even said that to see him was to see the Father. He meant this not in the sense that they are the same person, but in the sense that they are the same nature (John 10:30) and that the Father is in the Son and the Son in the Father. In John 5:18 we are told that his claim that God was "his own" Father was a claim to being "equal with God."

All writings should be interpreted according to context, and we should afford that same grace to Origen in this matter, allowing him to explain himself in the context of his own theological language and times. Thus, in the paragraph immediately preceding that cited by Kelly, Origen wrote:[25]

Moreover, nothing in the Trinity can be called greater or less, since the fountain of divinity alone contains all things by His word and reason, and by the Spirit of His mouth sanctifies all things which are worthy of sanctification, as it is written in the Psalm: "By the word of the Lord were the heavens strengthened, and all their power by the Spirit of His mouth." There is also a special working of God the Father, besides that by which He bestowed upon all things the gift of natural life. There is also a special ministry of the Lord Jesus Christ to those upon whom he confers by nature the gift of reason, by means of which they are enabled to be rightly what they are. There is also another grace of the Holy Spirit, which is bestowed upon the deserving, through the ministry of Christ and the working of the Father, in proportion to the merits of those who are rendered capable of receiving it.

In the context, three things are important. First, Origen affirmed the unity of the Godhead and the equality in nature of the Father, Son, and Spirit, saying "nothing in the Trinity can be called greater or less." Second, after affirming the equality of the three persons, he specified some of their respective functions. Third, the functions of which he spoke both here and in the passage cited by Kelly are all related to the work of God in and for believers. He was discussing the work of redemption, and pointing out the particular roles which Father, Son, and Spirit take in that work. To take the passage Kelly cited beyond that is to remove it from its context and apply it universally, whereas Origen surely meant it as applying to the topic of redemption.

Furthermore, in that passage he did not deny the work of the Son in the creation of things. There is good reason from the context to believe that Origen was speaking there only of rational beings, both in reference to their creation by the Father and their being made rational by the Son. In another instance, however, he clearly assigned the Son a role in the creation of all things. Immediately after commenting on John 1:1 and 2, he wrote, "This Son, accordingly, is also the truth and life of all things which exist. And with reason. For how could those things which were created live, unless they derived their being from life?"[26] When we note that this is in direct continuity with his comments on John 1:1 and 2, we must realize that he was explaining the verses that follow: "Through him all things were made; without him nothing was made that has been made"; and "In him was life, and that life was the light of men." Thus the Word has a double role in creation: being the working agent in creation, and giving life and rationality to all living and rational beings.

Also in respect of the incarnation, Origen taught that the Word, "divesting Himself of His equality with the Father,"[27] showed men the way of salvation. His teaching of the equality of Father and Son came forth strongly when he spoke of their omnipotence:

> And that you may understand that the omnipotence of the Father and Son is one and the same, as God and the Lord are one and the same with the Father, listen to the manner in which John speaks in the Apocalypse: "Thus saith the Lord God, which is, and which was, and which is to come, the Almighty." For who else was "He which is to come" than Christ? And as no one ought to be offended, seeing God is the Father, that the Saviour is also God; so also, since the Father is called omnipotent, no one ought to be offended that the Son of God is also called omnipotent.[28]

He included the Holy Spirit also in this unity when he wrote, "From which it most clearly follows that there is no difference in the Trinity, but that which is called the gift of the Spirit is made known through the Son, and operated by God the Father. 'But all these worketh that one and the self-same Spirit, dividing to every one severally as He will.'"[29]

The emphasis by Origen on the different roles of Father, Son, and Spirit should not be taken as a sign of a strong subordinationist. It is true that later thinkers such as Aetius in the late third century (the teacher of Arius), and Arius and Eusebius of Nicomedia in the fourth, interpreted him that way. However, it must be recognized that he wrote primarily to confront the errors of Monarchianism, and so had to stress the distinction of persons more than the unity of substance. Whatever subordinationism there is in Origen is in function among the members of the Trinity, not in nature, and is purely voluntary on the part of the Son and the Spirit, not a necessity of their nature.

There were in the unorthodox concepts of the Trinity two fundamental errors, the one incipient and the other explicit. First, there was a view which seemed to divide the divine nature by teaching that the Son and Spirit are "emanations" in the gnostic sense. This view surfaced later in the teaching of Arius who—though he denied that calling the Son a second God inferior to and created by the Father was ditheism—certainly could not rightly escape the charge. The second error was much more pronounced. It was that many people so stressed the unity of the divine nature that they denied the distinction of the persons. The orthodox line lay right between these views: a sound affirmation of the divine nature's unity and indivisibility, and a clear statement of the distinction of the equally perfectly divine persons. The greatest battle between the orthodox view and that which divided the nature of deity was to come in the fourth century with the Arian controversies.

CREEDAL GROWTH IN THE ANTE-NICENE PERIOD

Philip Schaff gave a number of instances in the New Testament of things which appear to reflect creedal thinking of that time. He included: John 1:50, the confession of Nathanael; Matthew 16:16, the confession of Peter; John 6:68, another confession of Peter; John 20:28, the confession of Thomas; Matthew 28:19, the baptismal formula; Acts 8:37, the confession of the eunuch; 1 Corinthians 8:6, the statement concerning "one God and one Lord"; 1 Timothy 3:16, the reference to the mystery of godliness; Hebrews 6:1, 2, the phrase, "the elementary articles of faith." Whether every one of these can be thought to reflect solidified ways of expressing the faith is somewhat doubtful. Certainly we ought not to think so about John 20:28; Acts 8:37; or John 1:50. The others, however, seem quite surely either to have been already solidified constructions or to have become such within a few generations. To this may be added 1 Corinthians 15:1–8 (Paul's definition of the gospel), and perhaps the *kenosis* passage in Philippians 2:6–12. As we saw earlier, the baptismal formula of Matthew 28:19 is reflected in the *Didache* and in other writings.

It seems that most organized statements of faith after the New Testament incorporate two main elements: the threefold reference to the Godhead, naming the Father, the Son, and the Holy Spirit, and a recitation of the work of Christ in saving sinners, outlined especially in 1 Corinthians 15:1–8.

The three points emphasized in this passage are that Christ died, was buried, and rose from the dead, (1 Cor. 15:3, 4). These central points in the work of redemption, plus the nature of the Godhead expressed in terms of unity and threefoldness, based on Matthew 28:19, are the basis of the creeds and statements of faith which came later.

Ignatius of Antioch (A.D. 107). The first statement of faith with which we are concerned is that of Ignatius of Antioch. Though it contains no reference to the Holy Spirit, it does speak of the Father and Son on equal terms, and concentrates on the work of redemption:

> Be deaf, therefore, when any would speak to you apart from (at variance with) JESUS CHRIST [the Son of God], who was descended from the family of David, born of Mary, who truly was born [both of God and of the Virgin . . . truly took a body; for the Word became flesh and dwelt among us without sin . . .], ate and drank [truly], truly suffered persecution under Pontius Pilate, was truly [and not in appearance] crucified and died . . . who was also truly raised from the dead [and rose after three days], his Father raising him up . . . [and after having spent forty days with the Apostles, was received up to the Father, and sits on his right hand, waiting till his enemies are put under his feet].[30]

The concentration here is clearly on the redemptive work of Christ and on fighting the docetism of Ignatius' time by stressing the reality of Christ's human nature.

Irenaeus of Lyons and Rome (A.D. 180). Irenaeus gave three forms of the statement of faith in three different contexts in *Against Heresies,* showing the variety of ways that the faith could be expressed in his day:

> First Form: The Church . . . has received from the Apostles . . . the faith . . . IN ONE GOD, THE FATHER ALMIGHTY, who made the heaven and the earth, and the seas, and all that in them is; and IN ONE CHRIST JESUS, THE SON OF GOD, who became flesh for our salvation; and IN THE HOLY GHOST, who through the prophets

preached the dispensations and the advent. . .and the birth from the Virgin, and the passion, and the resurrection from the dead, and the bodily assumption into heaven of the beloved Christ Jesus, our Lord, and his appearing from heaven in the glory of the Father, to comprehend all things under one head, and to raise up all flesh of all mankind, that, according to the good pleasure of the Father invisible, every knee of those that are in heaven and on the earth and under the earth should bow before Christ Jesus, our Lord and God and Saviour and King, and that every tongue should confess to him, and that he may execute righteous judgment over all: sending into eternal fire the spiritual powers of wickedness, the angels who transgressed and apostatized, and the godless and unrighteous and lawless and blasphemous among men, and granting life and immortality and eternal glory to the righteous and holy, who have both kept the commandments and continued in his love, some from the beginning, some after their conversion (I.X.1).

Second Form: Believing IN ONE GOD, Maker of heaven and earth, and all that in them is, Through CHRIST JESUS THE SON OF GOD; Who, for his astounding love towards his creatures, sustained the birth of the Virgin, himself uniting his manhood to God, and suffered under Pontius Pilate, and rose again, and was received in glory, shall come in glory, the Saviour of those who are saved, and the Judge of those who are judged; and sending into eternal fire the perverters of the truth and the despisers of his Father and his advent (III. iv. 1, 2).

Third Form: IN ONE GOD ALMIGHTY, from whom are all things; and IN THE SON OF GOD, JESUS CHRIST, our Lord, by whom are all things, and in his dispensations, through which the Son of God became man; the firm persuasion also IN THE SPIRIT OF GOD, who furnishes us with a knowledge of the truth, and has set forth the dispensations of the Father and the Son, in virtue of which he dwells in every generation of men, according to the will of the Father (IV. xxiii. 7).

Tertullian of Carthage (A.D. *200*). The great defender against Monarchianism also set forth three basic forms of the rule of faith, all intimately connected with the work of salvation which he saw as central to the gospel (*On the Veiling of Virgins*, 1; *Against Praxeas*, 2; *The Prescription Against Heretics*, 13):

First Form: The Rule of Faith is altogether one, sole, immovable, and irreformable—namely, to believe IN ONE GOD ALMIGHTY, the Maker of the World; and HIS SON, JESUS CHRIST, born of the Virgin Mary, crucified under Pontius Pilate, on the third day raised again from the dead, received in the heavens, sitting now at the right hand of the Father, coming to judge the quick and the dead, also through the resurrection of the flesh.

Second Form: But we believe always, and now more, being better instructed by the Paraclete, the Leader into all truth, ONE GOD: but under this dispensation which we call economy, and the SON of the one GOD, his Word [Logos] who proceeded from him, by whom all things were made, and without whom nothing was made. This was sent from the Father into the Virgin, and was born of her, both Man and God, the Son of Man and the Son of God, and called JESUS CHRIST: He suffered, he died and was buried, according to the Scriptures; and raised again by the Father, and taken up into the heavens, and sitteth at the right hand of the Father, he shall come to judge the quick and the dead: He thence did send, according to his promise, from the Father, the HOLY GHOST, the Paraclete, the Sanctifier of the faith of those who believe in the Father and the Son and the Holy Ghost.

Third Form: The Rule of Faith is, . . . namely, that by which we believe That there is but ONE GOD, and no other besides the Maker of the World, who produced the universe out of nothing, by his Word sent forth first of all; that this Word, called HIS SON, was seen in the name of God in various ways by the patriarchs, was always heard in the prophets, at last was sent down, from the Spirit and power of God the Father, into the Virgin Mary, was made flesh in her womb, and born of her, lived (appeared) as JESUS CHRIST; that then he preached the new law and the new promise of the kingdom of heaven; wrought miracles; was nailed to the cross; rose again on the third day; was caught up to the heavens; and sat down at the right hand of the Father; sent in his place the power of the HOLY GHOST, to guide the believers; he will come again with glory to take the saints into the enjoyment of eternal life and the celestial promises, and to judge the wicked with eternal fire, after the resuscitation (resurrection) of both, with the restitution (restoration) of the flesh.

Cyprian of Carthage (A.D. 250). Cyprian arranged the following brief statement as a response for the convert to Christianity to the question, "What do you believe?" prior to his baptism (*Epistle to Magnus,* 69, cf. 76):

I believe in GOD THE FATHER, in his SON CHRIST, in the HOLY GHOST. I believe in the forgiveness of sins, and eternal life through the holy Church.

Novatian of Rome (A.D.. 250). Novatian wrote this "rule of faith" in opposition to the heresies of his day, particularly against those which denied the unity of the Father and Son as the one God (*Treatise Concerning the Trinity*):

> The rule of truth demands that, first of all, we believe in GOD THE FATHER and Almighty Lord, that is, the most perfect Maker of all things. . . . The same rule of truth teaches us to believe, after the Father, also in the SON OF GOD, CHRIST JESUS, our Lord God, but the Son of God. . . . Moreover, the order of reason and the authority of faith, in due consideration of the words and Scriptures of the Lord, admonishes us, after this, to believe also in the HOLY GHOST, promised of old to the Church, but granted in the appointed and fitting time.

Origen of Alexandria (ca. A.D.. 230). By the time of Origen's writing, the Old and New Testaments were generally accepted throughout the Church as the supreme rule of faith. But the diversity of interpretations demanded that there be some regulatory statement accepted by the Church at large which should be used in instruction of converts and disciples. He produced what he called this generally accepted rule of faith throughout the Church in his *de Principiis* (*On the Principles*) Preface 4:

> The form of those things which are manifestly delivered by the preaching of the Apostles is this: First, that there is ONE GOD, who created and

79

framed every thing, and who, when nothing was, brought all things into being—God from the first creation and forming of the world, the God of all the just—Adam, Abel, Seth, Enos, Enoch, Noah, Shem, Abraham, Isaac, Jacob, the twelve Patriarchs, Moses, and the Prophets: and that this God, in the last days, as he had before promised through his Prophets, sent OUR LORD JESUS CHRIST, to all Israel first, and then, after the unbelief of Israel, also to the Gentiles. This just and good God, the Father of our Lord Jesus Christ, himself gave the Law and the Prophets and the Gospels, and he also is the God of the Apostles, and of the Old and New Testaments.

Then, secondly, that JESUS CHRIST himself, who came, was born of the Father before all creation. And when in the formation of all things he had served the Father (for by him all things were made), in these last times, emptying himself, he became man incarnate, while he was God, and though made man, remained God as he was before. He took a body like our body, differing in this point only, that it was born of the Virgin and the Holy Ghost. And since this Jesus Christ was born and suffered in truth, and not in appearance, he bore the death common to all men and truly died; for he truly rose from the dead, and after his resurrection, having conversed with his disciples, he was taken up.

They also delivered that the HOLY GHOST was associated in honor and dignity with the Father and the Son.

Gregory Thaumaturgus of Neo-Caesarea (ca. A.D. 270). A pupil of Origen and certainly one of the most profound thinkers in the early Church, Gregory Thaumaturgus wrote this creed which is more explicit on the doctrine of the Trinity than any other ante-Nicene rule of faith:

> There is ONE GOD, THE FATHER of the living Word, who is the substantive wisdom and eternal power and image of God: the perfect origin (begetter) of the perfect (begotten): the Father of the only-begotten Son.
>
> There is ONE LORD, one of one (only of the only), God of God, the image and likeness of the Godhead, the mighty Word, the wisdom which comprehends the constitution of all things, and the power which produces all creation; the true Son of the true Father, Invisible of Invisible, and Incorruptible of Incorruptible, and Immortal of Immortal, and Everlasting of Everlasting.
>
> And there is ONE HOLY GHOST, having his existence from God, and being manifested by the Son, namely, to men, the perfect likeness of the perfect Son, Life, the cause of the living [the sacred fount], sanctity, the Leader of sanctification: in whom is revealed God the Father, who is over all things and in all things, and God the Son, who is through all things: a perfect Trinity, not divided nor differing in glory and eternity and sovereignty.
>
> Neither, indeed, is there any thing created or subservient in the Trinity, nor introduced, as though not there before but coming in afterwards; nor, indeed, has the Son ever been without the Father, nor the Spirit without the Son, but the Trinity is ever the same, unvarying and unchangeable.

Lucian of Antioch (A.D. 300). This creed of Lucian presents a vivid statement of the orthodox doctrine of the

Trinity, while avoiding most of the vocabulary which later became the center of much of the Arian controversy, and especially the semi-Arian controversy, of the fourth century (from Athanasius, *Letter to the Synods of Ariminium and Seleucia*, Section 23):

> We believe, in accordance with evangelic and apostolic tradition, in ONE GOD THE FATHER ALMIGHTY, the Maker and Provider of all things.
>
> And in ONE LORD JESUS CHRIST, his Son, the only-begotten God, through whom all things were made, who was begotten of the Father before all ages, God of God, Whole of Whole, One of One, Perfect of Perfect, King of King, Lord of Lord, the living Word, Wisdom, Life, True Light, Way, Truth, Resurrection, Shepherd, Door, unchangeable and unalterable, the immutable likeness of the Godhead, both of the substance and will and power and glory of the Father, the first-born of all creation, who was in the beginning with God, the Divine Logos, according to what is said in the gospel: "And the Word was God," through whom all things were made, and in whom "all things consist:" who in the last days came down from above, and was born of a Virgin, according to the Scriptures, and became man, the Mediator between God and man, and the Apostle of our Faith, and the Prince of life; as he says, "I have come down from heaven, not to do mine own will, but the will of him that sent me:" who suffered for us, and rose for us the third day, and ascended into heaven and sitteth on the right hand of the Father, and again is coming with glory and power to judge the quick and the dead.
>
> And in THE HOLY GHOST given for consolation and sanctification and perfection to those

who believe; as also our Lord Jesus Christ commanded his disciples, saying, "Go ye, teach all nations, baptizing them in the name of the Father, and of the Son, and of the Holy Ghost;" clearly of the Father who is really a Father, and of a Son who is really a Son, and of the Holy Ghost who is really a Holy Ghost; these names being assigned not vaguely nor idly, but indicating accurately the special personality, order, and glory of those named, so that in Personality they are three, but in harmony one.

Having then this faith (from the beginning and holding it to the end) before God and Christ we anathematize all heretical false doctrine. And if any one, contrary to the right faith of the Scriptures, teaches and says that there has been a season or time or age before the Son of God was begotten, let him be accursed. And if any one says that the Son is a creature as one of the creatures, or generated as one of the things generated, or made as one of the things made, and not as the divine Scriptures have handed down each of the forenamed statements; or if a man teaches or preaches any thing else contrary to what we have received, let him be accursed.

For we truly and clearly both believe and follow all things from the holy Scriptures that have been transmitted to us by the Prophets and Apostles.

This is the final creed of the third century. Although it is dated A.D. 300, it surely was composed sometime shortly prior to then. It shows a thoroughly developed doctrine of the Trinity despite its avoidance of such terms as ὁμοούσιος. It was even suggested, at the Council of Antioch in A.D. 341, that this should replace the obnoxious Nicene Creed, for the precise terminology of the Nicene Creed made it difficult for many to accept the wording, while they surely accepted its substance (thus many of the ὁμοιούσιαν proponents following the Council of Nicea).

✓ The common thread throughout creedal development is the combination of the threefold reference to the Godhead and the summation of the work of redemption accomplished by Christ. If we were correct in our earlier discussion of the doctrine of the Trinity in the New Testament, we will have arrived at the beginning of the fourth century with statements of faith which are all essentially the same in substance. Though some are written with new vocabulary to fend off misinterpretation, others use a vocabulary derived from that of the New Testament. The continuity of trinitarian teaching in the early Church is thus seen to be unbroken.

We examine now, for the sake of continuity, a number of the creeds of the fourth century.

***Eusebius of Caesarea* (A.D. 325).** The following creed was submitted at the Council of Nicea before the Emperor Constantine, and suggested as the creed to be adopted at Nicea. It was, in fact, adopted substantially as it was presented by Eusebius, except for the addition of the famous ὁμοούσιον phrase.

> We believe in ONE GOD THE FATHER Almighty, Maker of all things visible and invisible; And in ONE LORD JESUS CHRIST, the Word of God, God of God, Light of Light, Life of Life, the only-begotten Son, the first-born of every creature, begotten of God the Father before all ages, by whom also all things were made; who for our salvation was made flesh and made his home among

84

men; and suffered; and rose on the third day; and ascended to the Father; and will come again in glory, to judge the quick and the dead. [We believe] also in ONE HOLY GHOST. We believe that each of these is and exists, the Father truly Father, and the Son truly Son, and the Holy Ghost truly Holy Ghost; even as our Lord, when sending forth his disciples to preach, said: "Go and make disciples of all nations, baptizing them into the name of the Father, and of the Son, and of the Holy Ghost."

Arius of Alexandria (A.D. 328). This brief creed was presented to the Emperor Constantine, at his request, and was an attempt by Arius to win his way back into good favor with the Church as a whole. Schaff noted that "It is heretical not by what it says, but by what it omits."[31] The denial of the true deity of Christ and the Holy Spirit is simply ignored in this statement. Nothing stands here which would contradict the Nicene faith, but neither is there anything to contradict what Arius had earlier taught and which, in ensuing controversies, it became clear that he continued to believe. Its inferiority in precision to other creeds of the time, not to mention its lack in orthodoxy, is readily apparent. It was a creed made to be misinterpreted, for Arius hoped by this to hide from Constantine his denial of true trinitarian faith.

> We believe in ONE GOD, the Father Almighty; And in THE LORD JESUS CHRIST, his Son, who was begotten of him before all ages, the Divine Logos, through whom all things were made, both those in the heavens and those on the earth; who came down and was made flesh; and suffered; and rose again; and ascended to the heavens; and shall come again to judge the quick and the dead. And

in THE HOLY GHOST; and in the resurrection of the flesh; and in the life of the world to come; and in a kingdom of heaven; and in one Catholic Church of God which extends to the ends of the earth.

Cyril of Jerusalem (ca. A.D. 350). Once an advocate of the ὁμοιούσιαν (of like nature, as opposed to ὁμοούσιος, of the same nature) formula, Cyril of Jerusalem recognized that what divided the *homoeousians* from the *homoousians* was not so much something substantive in belief, but something which concerned vocabulary alone. There were those among the *homoeousians* who adopted that word simply because it was more respectable than believing true Arianism, but whose beliefs differed little if any from those of Arius. Cyril's doctrine of the Trinity conforms in meaning to the doctrine set forth at Nicea, even if his words are not the same. There are two forms of his creed.

Long Form: We believe in ONE GOD THE FATHER Almighty, Maker of heaven and earth, and of all things visible and invisible; And in ONE LORD JESUS CHRIST, the only-begotten Son of God, begotten of the Father before all ages, very God, by whom all things were made; who appeared in the flesh, and became man [of the Virgin and the Holy Ghost]; was crucified and was buried; rose on the third day; and ascended into heaven, and sitteth on the right hand of the Father; and will come again in glory, to judge the quick and the dead; of whose kingdom there shall be no end. And in ONE HOLY GHOST, the Advocate, who spake in the Prophets. And in one baptism of repentance for the remission of sins; and in one holy Catholic Church; and in the resurrection of the flesh, and in life everlasting.

The shorter form was almost certainly used simply as an affirmation for new converts immediately prior to their baptism:

> Short Form: I believe in the Father, and in the Son, and in the Holy Ghost, and in one baptism of repentance.

Epiphanius of Constantia (A.D. 374). The two creeds of Epiphanius were written at the request of presbyters to expound the Nicene faith in opposition to the revival of Arianism at that time. His statements lead directly to the final form of the Nicene Creed, accepted at Constantinople in A.D. 381. They show almost verbal agreement.

> First Creed: We believe in ONE GOD THE FATHER Almighty, Maker of heaven and earth, and of all things visible and invisible; And in ONE LORD JESUS CHRIST, the only-begotten Son of God, begotten of the Father before all worlds, that is, of the substance of the Father, Light of Light, very God of very God, begotten, not made, being of one substance (consubstantial) with the Father; by whom all things were made, both those in the heavens and those on earth; who for us men, and for our salvation, came down from heaven, and was incarnate by the Holy Ghost and the Virgin Mary, and was made man; He was crucified for us under Pontius Pilate, and suffered, and was buried; and the third day He rose again, according to the Scriptures; and ascended into heaven, and sitteth on the right hand of the Father; and he shall come again, with glory, to judge the quick and the dead; of whose kingdom shall be no end; And in THE HOLY GHOST, the Lord, and Giver of life, who proceedeth from the Father, who with the Father

and the Son together is worshipped and glorified, who spake by the Prophets; in one holy Catholic and Apostolic Church; we acknowledge one baptism for remission of sins; and we look for the resurrection of the dead; and the life of the world to come. But to those who say, "There was a time when he was not," and, "He was not before he was begotten," or, "He was made of nothing [of things that are not]," or "of another substance or essence," saying that the Son of God is effluent or variable, these the Catholic and Apostolic Church anathematizes.

The longer form of Epiphanius' creed, while it agrees in full with the shorter form, adds material concerning the nature of the union of God and man in the Incarnate Logos—what later became known as the hypostatic union, the union of two complete and perfect natures in one hypostasis, or person. It also changes the wording of the description of the Holy Spirit slightly, and adds the word "uncreated" in reference to him. We do not quote it here, since aside from what has been noted, it is a repetition of the shorter form.

The Nicene Creed (A.D. 325 and 381). This brings us past the time of the first form of the Nicene Creed, adopted at the Council of Nicea, A.D. 325, and within seven years of the second and longer form, adopted at the Council of Constantinople, A.D. 381. It is readily seen that for some time the entire substance of the Nicene Creed has been latent in the creeds and statements of faith of the earlier years. Even the word ὁμοούσιος was used at least a century earlier by Origen. It is not so much what was said at Nicea and Constantinople that was new as *how* it was said. We present both forms in parallel columns in order best to see the slight changes between them:

Nicea, A.D. 325	Constantinople, A.D. 381
We believe in one God, the FATHER Almighty, Maker of all things visible and invisible.	We believe in one God, the FATHER Almighty, Maker of heaven and earth, and of all things visible and invisible.
And in one Lord JESUS CHRIST, the Son of God, begotten of the Father [the only-begotten; that is, of the essence of the Father, God of God], Light of Light, very God of very God, begotten, not made, being of one substance (ὀμοούσιον) with the Father; by whom all things were made [both in heaven and on earth]; who for us men, and for our salvation, came down and was incarnate and was made man; he suffered, and the third day he rose again, ascended into heaven; from thence he shall come to judge the quick and the dead.	And in one Lord JESUS CHRIST, the only-begotten Son of God, begotten of the Father before all worlds (æons), Light of Light, very God of very God, begotten, not made, being of one substance with the Father; by whom all things were made; who for us men, and for our salvation, came down from heaven, and was incarnate by the Holy Ghost of the Virgin Mary, and was made man; he was crucified under Pontius Pilate, and suffered, and was buried, and the third day he rose again, according to the Scriptures, and ascended into heaven, and sitteth on the right hand of the Father; from thence he shall come again, with glory, to judge the quick and the dead; whose kingdom shall have no end.
And in the HOLY GHOST.	And in the HOLY GHOST, the Lord and Giver of life, who proceedeth from the Father, who with the Father and the Son together is worshiped and glorified, who spake by the prophets. In one holy Catholic and apostolic Church; we acknowledge one baptism for the remission of

sins; we look for the resurrection of the dead, and the life of the world to come.

[But those who say: 'There was a time when he was not;' and 'He was not before he was made;' or 'He was made out of nothing,' or 'He is of another substance' or 'essence,' or 'The Son of God is created,' or 'changeable,' or 'alterable'—they are condemned by the holy catholic and apostolic Church.]

We have traced creedal development now through the Council of Constantinople, A.D. 381, and have seen that the content believed by those writing the creeds has remained, apparently, the same (except for those such as Arius who were recognized as unorthodox) regarding the doctrine of the Trinity, even if the words differed. It is necessary to understand the key words of the controversy in order to understand the fourth-century developments of the doctrine.

THE VOCABULARY OF TRINITARIANISM

The word "Trinity" has a rather long history behind it by the time of the fourth century. The earliest extant usage is from Theophilus, ca. A.D. 170, and that usage showed clear signs of being commonplace at the time. We may assume that the word had been used one to three or four decades earlier, during the first half of the second century. The earliest Latin use of the word is by Tertullian, A.D. 190 to 200, by which time it has clearly become a solidly entrenched theological term. It has come to stand for that conception of the Godhead which affirms equally the unity of the substance of deity and the triunity of the persons.

There are several other terms, however, which entered trinitarian discussion, and were of great importance:

Homoousios. This word became the shibboleth of Nicene orthodoxy when it was introduced into the Creed at Nicea by Constantine, at the insistence of Hosius, the Spanish bishop who presided at the Council. The creed had been suggested by Eusebius of Caesarea. The term, as we noted before, was used at least as early as Origen, probably sometime in the first three decades of the third century, and seems to be used by him as an accepted term. The term means *of one substance.* Its implications for theology are far-reaching and of greatest import. This term was the object of constant controversy brought about by misinterpretation among those who opposed its use but were in favor of the concept it taught. Others practiced total rejection of both the term and the intended concept. Those who misinterpreted the term were primarily orthodox in their idea of the Trinity. That is, they believed firmly that three distinct persons were the same God. These were the *homoeousians*, also called semi-Arians, who taught that the three persons of the Trinity were of "like" substance, rather than "one substance." The idea that the *homoeousians* and *homoousians* were driving at was the same: that three persons were equally the same God. But each side misunderstood the other. The *homoousians*, on the one hand, thought that the *homoeousians* denied the unity of the three persons, a position which they considered tantamount to tritheism. The *homoeousians*, on the other hand, thought that the *homoousians* denied the distinction of the persons, a position which they knew was Monarchian, particularly close to modalistic Monarchianism. One of the Nicene defenders, Marcellus of Ancyra,

91

actually did go so far as to become modalistic, but most did not. The key to the matter was in recognizing that the two groups meant the same thing by the two terms, that the three persons, though distinct as to personality, were the same as to deity.

The other group which opposed the use of ὁμοούσιος, of course, was the truly Arian party. They understood precisely what the word meant and how it was used, and they rejected the concept, not only the term. They believed that the Son of God was actually of a second and completely different substance from the Father, created by the Father, not eternal, and certainly not true deity. Though, because of his role in creation, the Son was given the privilege of being called "God." He could not be called "the God."

The shibboleth of Nicene orthodoxy was thus both a success and a failure. It succeeded in bringing the real foe out into the open and making it impossible for him to hide his heresy any longer. It failed in that it divided the essentially orthodox party into two camps, thus weakening its influence on the Church. It was only through the careful discussion of this and the next term at the Council of Alexandria (A.D. 362) by Athanasius and a number of *homoeousian* thinkers that saved orthodoxy from a permanent split over vocabulary.

Hypostasis. This word has a long and complex history in Greek thought which is beyond the bounds of the present study. Etymologically, it means "that which stands under" whatever is the subject of investigation. In this sense it is precisely parallel to the Latin *substantia*; and like "substance," it had many idiomatic meanings which were far from philosophical. It was used for goods or possessions either of monetary or real value. It was also used for the underlying character of an individual. Mostly it was used for two concepts, "substance" and "person." And this is precisely what caused the trouble. The old school of Greek theologians in the fourth century used the term as an equivalent for οὐσία or *substantia*; the new school used it as the equivalent of *persona*. Confusion was bound to result. The new school accused the old school of modalism for claiming that there was only one hypostasis in the Godhead; but by this the old school meant that there was only one substance in the Godhead. The old school accused the new school of tritheism for claiming that there were three hypostases in the Godhead. Of course, by this the new school meant that there were three persons. The confusion was worked out at the Council of Alexandria in 362. There Athanasius, the leader of Nicene orthodoxy and the gallant defender of the ὁμοούσιον led an exchange of ideas about the two meanings of this word and their relation to the use of οὐσία and ὁμοούσιος, which was to prove the critical point in fourth-century trinitarianism. The parties at the Council realized that they were in agreement in concept, and agreed to accept each other's terminology so long as its meaning was understood and not violated. Thus those who spoke of three hypostases were welcome to do so, so long as they meant by it three persons, and that they in no sense denied the unity of the divine substance. Those who spoke of a single hypostasis were free to do so, so long as what they meant was a single substance, not a single person. Meanwhile, those who used ὁμοούσιος were at liberty to do so, so long as they used the term οὐσία as equivalent to the *old school's* conception of hypostasis (which, by the way, was the conception Athanasius favored. This would mean simply that they believed in a single substance of deity, while affirming the distinction of persons. But the homoousians must not mean by οὐσία what the *new school* meant by hypostasis, for that would mean that they taught a unity of person, which would be modalism all over again.

Prosōpon. The word πρόσωπον had originally been the term for "mask," and had been used to describe a role in a play, or the actor who might play the role, or as a term for "face." However, it also began to be used, around the first century B.C., for what we would call "person." One further usage of it was to describe a representative in court. The difficulty with this word was that all of these meanings continued in common use for centuries. When the word was used to discuss the Trinity, therefore, it was bound to cause trouble. If it were used with the connotation of a mask (perhaps even of a face), the idea would resemble that of the Hindu trinity of Brahma, Vishnu, and Shiva, the three aspects (in older Vedic religion) of the All, or Brahman. Used with the connotation of a role, it would take on the modalistic idea. Used with the connotation of a representative in court, it would take on the concept of the demigod of gnostic emanationalism and later Arianism. None of these would do. The word could only be accepted by orthodoxy if it were clearly used to mean "person." Fortunately, that was the meaning intended by most of those who used it. There were still difficulties, however. Those who used *prosōpon* for "person" almost invariably used *hypostasis* for substance; so when they saw others using the phrase "three *hypostases*," they were convinced that these people were teaching tritheism. Those who spoke of three *hypostases*, on the other hand, thought that the proponents of *prosōpon* were teaching modalism when they insisted that there was in the Godhead only one *hypostasis*. The predictable debates over terminology happened again, and again they were ironed out, again primarily at the Council at Alexandria under the supervision of Athanasius.

Genētos, Agenētos; Gennētos, Agennētos. At the same time that there was confusion over the words for person and substance, there was confusion over terms for two other concepts also: begetting (or being begotten) and bringing into existence (or being brought into existence), and their negations. The difficulty here was aggravated by the extreme similarity of the words (note the single and double *n*). It is doubtful whether there was any difference between them at all when spoken. Not only was this a difficulty to the Fathers themselves in attempting to communicate with each other, it is a great hindrance to patristic research. Different manuscripts of the same writing differ from one another, and it is often nearly impossible to tell whether one word or the other is the original word in the text.

The orthodox concept, again, was clear, whether the terminology was or not. The Word, the Son of God, had surely been "begotten" and hence was *gennētos* (from γεννάω, to beget or bear); but he had not come into existence at any time, for he was eternal: hence he was *agenētos* ("without a beginning," from γίνομαι, to bring into existence). If this were all there was to it, there would not have been such a problem. The problem came from the realization that the one person (whether one used *hypostasis* or *prosōpon*) of the Word, the Son, had taken on a second nature. He had become man, while he remained God. This meant that one of the two natures of the Word was γένητος; that is, he had come into existence, and was γέννητος (begotten), while the other nature was γέννητος (begotten) but ἀγένητος (not brought into existence, not created). A further dilution of the proper meaning arose, at least of the word γεννάω, so that it began in some writings to take on the same meaning as γίνομαι, and it too was used for "to bring into existence." The importance of the distinction between the words was graphically illustrated by the fact that Athanasius devoted an entire chapter of his first *Discourse Against the Arians* to the subject. The state of the confusion of the words at that time is illustrated by one paragraph of that discussion:

> But if they ask according as Asterius ruled it, as if 'what is not a work but was always' were unoriginate, then they must constantly be told that the Son as well as the Father must . . . in this sense be called unoriginate [ἀγέννητος, in both instances!]. For He is neither in the number of things originated, nor a work, but has ever been with the Father, as has already been shewn, in spite of their many variations for the sole sake of speaking against the Lord, 'He is of nothing' and 'He was not before His generation.' When then, after failing at every turn, they betake themselves to the other sense of the question, 'existing but not generated of any nor having a father,' we shall tell them that the unoriginate [ἀγέννητος] is only one, namely the Father; and they will gain nothing by their question (Discourse Against Arius, IX. 31).

The solution to this problem came late in the fourth century with the general consensus of orthodoxy that γεννάω would be used only for begetting, and γίνομαι for bringing into existence.

It was inevitable, of course, that another word should be associated with these two words: μονογενής, the word commonly translated "only-begotten." It is used of Christ in John 1:18, the "only-begotten" God, and in John 3:16 the "only-begotten" Son, and hence its authority as a description of the Son was unimpeachable. This caused a problem for those holding trinitarian conceptions in that they thought the word derived directly from γεννάω and many of them (especially all the Arians) had begun to believe that γεννάω meant not only "to beget" but also "to bring into existence."

Of course, if γεννάω really did mean "to bring into existence," and if μονογενής really did derive from it, that would be the end of the doctrine of the Trinity. Like so many other terminological problems, this was solved through careful discussion among participants, in which they agreed that they would use γεννάω for "to beget," not for "to bring into existence," and γίνομαι for "to bring into existence," not for "to beget." This allowed them to continue to apply μονογενής to Christ, thinking as they did that it was a form of γεννάω, not of γίνομαι. Thus the temporary correlation among the Church Fathers of γεννάω and γίνομαι ended.

Unfortunately, much of the debate over μονογενής could have been avoided had the Church Fathers had the facilities for advanced lexicographical study. Unknown to the Church Fathers of the orthodox party, the word μονογενής actually meant exactly what they were trying to say of Christ: that he is *unique* in *his* relation to God, having a relation which no created thing has. The word was derived from neither γίνομαι nor γεννάω, but from γένος, "kind." Hence it meant "only one of its kind." The danger in Arianism was not only that it made Christ a creature, but that it threatened to rob him of his unique position as the only possible Savior. Rousas J. Rushdoony notes:

> . . .Christ is eliminated by Arius. Although called the greatest of creatures, He is still a creature. Arius' Jesus cannot know God and therefore cannot reveal Him. And, although Arius' Jesus or Son cannot be surpassed, i.e., his god (sic) cannot create a superior one, still he can create one equal to the Son. The door is thus thrown wide open to other sons of god to rank equally high with god, and, because of their timeliness in history, rank higher than Jesus with men.[32]

Substantia. Besides the Greek terms involved in the controversy, there were two major Latin words involved. The first is *substantia*. Although the word was used idiomatically to mean "goods" or "property," and in a legal sense to denote "that to which two or more parties could share legal claim," there was never much doubt as to what the Fathers intended when using *substantia* in trinitarian discussion. For them divine *substantia* was simply the being of God. Thus to say, with the Latin orthodox theologians, that Father, Son, and Spirit were *consubstantialis* was to say that they shared the same basic "thing" or "what" that they were: namely, they were God.

One further logical step was necessary to reach the conclusion that they were all the one same God: that the *substantia* of God was infinite and indivisible. This was agreed on by all sides, including the Arians. Hence for the orthodox to prove that the persons were consubstantial was to prove that they were the same God. It was partly because they thought that assigning the same substance to three distinct persons meant a division in that substance that the Arians resisted both the term "consubstantial" (or ὁμοούσιος; οὐσία was used as synonymous for *substantia*) and the concept which it represented. They failed to see, as did the orthodox Fathers, that substance and personality were different levels of being. In Aristotelian terms they might be called categories, though Aristotle did not specify a category called "person." Thus three persons could share equally in (or inhere equally in) one substance, the substance remaining undivided.

Persona. A term with as long and complicated a background as πρόσωπον, *persona* shared many meanings with the Greek term. The two were often used to translate each other. Its original meaning was primarily that of "mask" or "role," and it went through much the same development that the Greek word did. It came to mean not only the role that an actor played, but the actor himself. It, too, was used in legal terminology to denote the court representative either of the plaintiff or the defendant. And, just like πρόσωπον, *persona* came to mean an individual agent, a "person." The Latin Fathers, then, would speak of three *personæ* in the one *substantia* of deity, while the Greeks would speak of three πρόσωπα (and later of three ὑποστάσεις) in the one οὐσία (and the earlier Greeks could also use "one ὑπόστασις," as did the old school of fourth-century Greeks). Of course, when with the later Greek Fathers ὑπόστασις replaced πρόσωπον as the primary word for "person," then persona was used to translate ὑπόστασις.

A word which was connected with both *substantia* and *persona* was *subsistentia*. Its history is like that of ὑπόστασις, which early meant simply "substance," but later changed to mean "person" or individual "agent." Thus the pattern we saw with the Greeks, we see again with the Latins. The earlier Latins would speak of one *subsistentia*, using it as nearly equivalent to *substantia* (and hence οὐσία), and the later Latins spoke of three *subsistentia*, making it equivalent to *persona* (and hence to πρόσωπον and the later ὑπόστασις) in one *substantia*. During part of the time there was an overlap of terms, just as with the Greeks.

The Latin did not present such problems with the concepts of begetting (*generare*) and making (*facere*) as the Greek did. For the Latins it was simple enough to say that the Word was *genitum, non factum*, which meant clearly, begotten, not made, generated, not brought into existence.

III

FOURTH-CENTURY TRINITARIANISM AND THE ARIAN CONTROVERSY

THE question is often asked how those committed to religion, regardless what religion, can consider it appropriate for there to be real "conflicts" in Christianity. Did not the founder of this great movement say "Peace I leave with you; my peace I give you. I do not give to you as the world gives. Do not let your hearts be troubled and do not be afraid" (John 14:27). What is the sense in quarrelling over differences in belief? There are two possible answers to this question.

First, it may be said that there is no sense to such quarrels, and that debate of religious ideas should be kept entirely on the intellectual plane and should not be made a source of "battle," whether physical or verbal. Religious ideas should be kept in the purely rational sphere. They should not be the source of division among people.

There is much to be said for this view. As much as possible we should attempt to keep differences in religious beliefs from causing strife. Love must cross the lines of religious diversity. If while we were yet sinners and alienated from God, Christ became a man and died for our sins, should we not follow his command to

103

"love our enemies"? Religious discussions should be carried on in as calm a manner as possible. We must remember that we are human, and all disagreements in areas which we hold important will raise our emotions somewhat. One need only think of two men arguing over which is the better football team, or the better car, to see that the nature of humans is to become emotionally aroused when we disagree strongly with one another. In short, all religious differences should be handled in the most loving, kind, peaceful manner possible.

Yet there is an appropriate place for conflict in religion. Those who say this, however, are usually the first to say that conflict is to be avoided if at all possible, without sacrificing whatever principles are considered more important than peace and unity and fellowship. These people believe that even such conflict is itself an expression of love.

The former position often sees religion more as a set of philosophical ideas and speculations than as something of life or death importance. Many in this camp have a concept of love best characterized as sloppy sentimentality which avoids conflict not so much out of love for persons as out of selfish love for peaceful relations. They seem willing to compromise principles for the sake of harmonious relations.

Love is often very harsh—it must be so. The harsh disciplining of a child for a dangerous and disobedient act must not be seen as the parent's lack of love, but as a love of the highest sort—a love which sacrifices self and the self's harmonious relations for the good of the other. The love which made the Savior bleed is the same love which cleansed the temple.

Those who oppose religious conflict are convinced that the truth or falsity of religious beliefs really has nothing to do with the eternal (or even temporal) welfare of the people holding them. Those who are willing to "fight the good fight of the faith" (1 Tim. 6:12) believe that the truth or falsity of religious beliefs has everything to do with our welfare.

If real love cares most for the welfare of others, even above our harmonious relations with them, and if one believes true religious beliefs are essential to eternal or temporal welfare, then one must be willing to sacrifice harmony for truth. A good medical doctor denounces quacks. It is the only loving and right thing for a doctor to do if he believes the quacks are really not good for others. The man who is a religious apologist hopes with all his heart for peace and harmony now but is willing to sacrifice both of them for peace and harmony in eternity for others, not only for himself.

This kind of concern motivated Churchmen in the controversies of the early Church. They were certain that Peter was right when he said of Christ, "Neither is there salvation in any other: for there is none other name under heaven given among men, whereby we must be saved" (Acts 4:12).

The Churchmen of the fourth-century controversies, orthodox and heterodox alike, accepted this principle. Each side was sure that belief in true Christianity as they saw it was essential to salvation. There were no complaints of, "Why are you so upset? We only disagree over a matter of doctrine." Both sides thought that belief in the essential doctrines of Christianity was necessary for eternal well-being, and each seemed to know that the other side was doing what it did not out of hate, but out of a sincere love and compassion for its opponents. Even Athanasius, the most bitter enemy of Arius' teachings, when the thought occurred to him that some people might exult in the death of Arius, reacted simply with the words, "God forbid!"

It was almost inevitable that in the fiery conflicts of that time there should be hard feelings of the one side against the other. But the basic love of each side for the other was the prime motivation—not for compromise and a fallacious, outward harmony, but for debate of the highest order, designed to bring the otherside to a right relationship with God.

Love and a passion for truth were the primary motivations behind the conflict. This is not to say that there were none with purely political motives who sought only power, honor, and glory in front of the church. Surely there were some of these on each side. The important point here is that we recognize the legitimacy of religious conflict.

TRINITARIANISM AT THE INCEPTION OF THE FOURTH CENTURY

The first three centuries of trinitarian doctrinal development brought, on the orthodox side, primarily a change only in vocabulary, not in substance. On the heterodox side, however, it brought great changes in substance, some believing the three persons were no more than three roles or masks put on by one person, three modes in which the divine monad related to men. Others believed that the three were distinct beings, the Father the one true God, the Son his first and greatest creation, and the Holy Spirit yet another creation, first below the Son. Still others believed that the Trinity was the monad plus two emanations from it for the purpose of creation.

Each of these failed in some way to represent what we have seen—and what the orthodox Christians at the time saw—that the New Testament teaches about the Father, the Son, and Spirit. The orthodox Christians, in accord with Scripture, believed that Father, Son, and Spirit were distinct and coequal persons who were at the same time the same undivided substance of deity, the same God.

The fourth century saw a predictable continuation of these lines of thought. There remained those in the fourth century who were Monarchians, either dynamic or modalistic. They followed generally the teachings of Sabellius and Callistus, representatives of modalistic Monarchianism. The labors of Hippolytus, Tertullian, Novatian, and Origen, however, had made their mark, and Monarchianism never again enjoyed the strength it had in the third century.

Arianism also has its roots in the third century. The Antiochene school of theologians, the most important in the East at the time, rejected the doctrine of identity of substance of Father and Son at a synod in A.D. 268, and developed a strongly subordinationist view of the Son's relation to the Father. Lucian, one of the Antiochene leaders, became the teacher of Arius (A.D. 256-336) and of Eusebius of Nicomedia, who was a great defender of Arianism during and after the Council of Nicea; and it was from Antiochene subordinationism that Arianism grew.

The orthodox concept of the identity in substance of Father and Son was anathema to the Arians, for they believed the Son to be created out of nothing, while the Father's substance was the indivisible, eternal substance of deity. Arianism also rejected the deity of the Holy Spirit. The Spirit was considered to be God's force, not personal, and not God, but the power by which God worked in creation through the Logos.

OUTBREAK TO NICEA (A.D. 318-325)

Arius of Alexandria developed his teacher Lucian's subordinationism into a full-blown system of thought in which he denied the eternity of the Logos and both the personality and deity of the Holy Spirit. Apparently one day in A.D. 318, at a teaching session, Bishop Alexander of Alexandria was teaching on the eternity of the

107

Logos. Arius voiced his objection to the view, and after some days of debate, the presbyters of Alexandria agreed with Alexander. As a result, Arius, unconvinced of the orthodox position, was banned from the Alexandrian churches. He left the city and was well received by Eusebius of Nicomedia, whose theology agreed for the most part with his. Eusebius was a fellow student of Lucian of Antioch and of Eusebius of Caesarea. Although the theology of Eusebius of Caesarea was in fact opposed to Arius', his terminology did not agree with the main body of orthodoxy represented by Alexander. Eusebius of Caesarea therefore thought himself in agreement with Arius, though he later saw he was not.

The Eusebiuses both had strong ties with the Emperor Constantine through his wife and family, and appealed to him for help for Arius. Constantine talked with representatives of both sides of the controversy, especially with Bishop Hosius of Cordova, a close friend and longtime aide of Constantine who supported the orthodox viewpoint of Alexander. Apparently Constantine did not really understand the theological issues very well at first, if at all. But he did understand that this problem had caused a major division within Christianity; and as a Christian himself, he wished to see this brought to an end. He did all he could to restore unity without using political force, but to no avail.

Finally, in the spring of A.D. 325, Constantine, with the encouragement of bishops on both sides, called for a conference of the leading bishops throughout the empire to discuss this and other matters, mainly questions of ecclesiastical polity and the Church calendar. The Council met in Nicea, beginning in early May, and ending in late June. The theological matters were discussed and decided upon within the first two to three weeks of the meetings, a relatively short time compared with the time they spent on other matters, considering the gravity of the subject.

The role of the emperor in all this has long been the subject of great debate. It has been argued that his purpose was only political, the unification of a powerful force within the empire, namely the Christian Church. Christianity was growing rapidly and the Church had begun to include many higher class citizens. It is true, as Schaff said, that "the interference of imperial politics only poured oil on the flame, and embarrassed the natural course of the theological argument."[1] However, it seems highly questionable to see Constantine's involvement in the problem as purely political, or nearly so, as others have implied. The more likely view is that politics and religion were both important to Constantine, for it appears that he inherited from his father an early tendency toward Christianity, and certainly at his famous "conversion" something more than an ingenious plan for military victory occurred to him.

There is no room to question his commitment to Christianity later in his life, for his desire to be baptized was so strong that he still sought it during his dying days, and indeed received it from Eusebius of Nicomedia, removing the imperial robes and donning the white of the humble baptismal recipient. But while religious motivation was at least a large part of the reason for Constantine's calling the Council, we should not assume that he understood well the issues involved in the debate.

Constantine's own opinions were probably more Arian than orthodox, at least at the start of the controversy. But his real desire was simply to believe the Christian faith, and it was up to the Church to decide what that faith was. The fact that during the Council, probably at the suggestion of Hosius, he proposed the addition of the word ὁμοούσιος to the creed submitted by Eusebius of Caesarea, might make us think that he had begun to understand the issues, and had seen the truth of the orthodox position. This is possible, but not likely, for his later leanings were consistently Arian.

Arius had made his views plain to the Church long before the Council, in a letter to Alexander of Alexandria. Though far from clear in every respect, the letter showed that Arius denied the eternity of the Logos and considered him created. He also denied the consubstantiality of Father and Son.

Because of Arius' explicit airing of his views, the members of the Council were all familiar with his opinions before he even presented them there himself.

The Arians first presented a creed of their own. Whether this was actually authored by Arius is not known, nor is it certain whether he himself presented it to the Council. The Arian creed was roundly rejected by the vast majority of the attendees. Arius apparently left the Council at that time, or was forced to leave. Eusebius of Nicomedia became the main defender of Arianism during the rest of the meetings.

Following that, Eusebius of Caesarea, a friend of Arius, proposed a creed to the council:

> We believe in one God, the Father, Almighty, Maker of all things visible and invisible. . . . and in one Lord, Jesus Christ, the Word of God, God of God, Light of light, Life of life, the only-begotten Son, born before all creation [πρωτότοκος; lit. "first-born," or "preeminent"], begotten of God the Father, before all ages, by whom also all things were made; who on account of our salvation became incarnate, and lived among men; and who suffered and rose again on the third day, and ascended to the Father, and shall come again in glory to judge the living and the dead. We believe also in the Holy Spirit. We believe in the existence and

subsistence of each of these [persons]: that the Father is truly Father, the Son truly Son, and the Holy Spirit truly Holy Spirit; even as our Lord also, when he sent forth his disciples to preach the Gospel, said, "Go and teach all nations, baptizing them in the name of the Father, and of the Son, and of the Holy Spirit." Concerning these doctrines we steadfastly maintain their truth, and avow our full confidence in them; such also have been our sentiments hitherto, and such we shall continue to hold until death. . . .[2]

This creed won the general approval of most of the participants at the Council. Its language was scriptural, it taught the deity of Christ, and it affirmed the personal distinctions of Father, Son, and Spirit. However, it did not prevent misinterpretation, and that is precisely what the Arian party did with it. Athanasius wrote that they actually sat and winked back and forth with each other, making hand signals and facial gestures, letting each other know of the different ways they could interpret this to fit their theology. Grant points out the problem, and its solution:

Scriptural language, however, was not necessarily orthodox, and the Alexandrians who dominated Nicaea were well aware that Arius found these terms acceptable. Left to their own devices, the Nicene leaders would never have allowed the council to accept the formulary Eusebius set forth. They would have preferred to tear it in shreds.

As it happened, however, they were not left to their own devices, for Constantine immediately intervened. He praised the declaration as "most orthodox," stated that it expressed his own belief, and urged the bishops to subscribe to it. In his view, only one more word was necessary. This was, of course, the famous *homoousios*, "of the same essence," used of the relation of the Son to the Father and already agreed upon by Ossius and Alexander.[3]

Though the participants probably would not have liked to "tear it in shreds," as Grant believes since they would have agreed with it, they certainly saw the weaknesses in it, and realized that it was in desperate need of some adjustments because of its ambiguity. Grant implied that the solution, using ὁμοούσιος, was primarily decided upon by Constantine. In this, as in most of his article, Grant attributed much more to Constantine than seems wise. It is surely true that Constantine is the one who formally suggested the term, but it is quite probable, if not certain, that he did so at the insistence, or at least the strong encouragement of Bishop Hosius and other orthodox leaders.

The term was not new, since it was used by Origen nearly a century before. It was commonplace in orthodox theology, but the object of great scorn from the Arians. Having seen the response of the orthodox to Arius' own creed, he knew that Arianism itself could not win at the Council. Witnessing the inevitable debates and discussions after the presentation by Eusebius, he saw what the orthodox were driving at as the weakness in Eusebius' document. Being close to Hosius and his allies, he knew they favored the term; and knowing the hatred of the term by the Arians, it seemed clear that this was precisely the term which was needed to perform what the orthodox wanted done—to make the creed of Eusebius impervious to Arian reinterpretation. It is difficult to imagine that Constantine himself thought independently of using the term, just as it is hard to believe that Constantine thoroughly understood all the theological issues surrounding him. The

112

term filled the need perfectly; it prohibited any Arian reinterpretations.

Following the formal suggestion of the term ὁμοούσιος, there erupted great debate at the Council. There were three parties: first, the true Arians were vastly outnumbered and never really amounted to a majority in the Church. In the next two or three centuries, the primary missionary activity in Gaul and Germany was done by descendants of the Arians, who later fled the southern part of the Roman Empire. But even then most of the "barbarian" Christians probably never heard of the controversy over the Trinity, holding to a very simple faith in the Father, Son, and Spirit. The second group, the true Nicenes, led by Alexander, Hosius, Eustathius, and Athanasius, numbered many more than the Arians, but still were fewer than the third party. The *homoeousians*, named for their advocacy of ὁμοιούσιος over ὁμοούσιος, were the large middle party, also called semi-Arians—an accurate description for only a small number of them. No doubt, most of them were orthodox in faith, even though their vocabulary was different. Probably only a few actually held the doctrines of Arius. Each party presented arguments to support its position.

As we noted before, the Arians used as their prime principle the absolute unity of the monad. They denied the possibility of any multiplicity in unity, a principle which destroyed the Christian answer to the philosophical problem of the one and the many. Orthodox Christianity believes that both unity and plurality characterize ultimate reality. Arianism sees only unity as ultimate. Though the Christians of that time, and probably the politicians as well, were not likely to see the socio-political implications in Arianism, and most did not see the destruction of the answer to the problem of the one and the many, Arianism did lead later to

113

difficulties in philosophy and politics. Arianism's emphasis on unity lent itself easily to the politics of unrestricted monarchy—despotism, in fact. Orthodoxy lent itself to division of powers in government.

The Arians were not confined to philosophical arguments. They used the Scriptures of both Testaments, and found in them much that they could interpret so as to support their theology. They used the passages in the Bible which spoke of the Son as begotten, interpreting this as meaning "brought into existence." Indeed, much of the philosophical use of γεννάω at the time had given it that meaning. Arius found this to be the perfect means of supporting his belief in the creation of the Son, and hence the belief that the Son was not co-eternal with the Father.

Arius appealed also to any Scripture passages which could be interpreted as subordinating the Son, making him subservient to the Father, describing him as changing in any manner, growing in knowledge, lacking in any knowledge, or having any weaknesses. Arius reasoned that if the Son were subject to such things he could not be truly God, but must be a created being. There were admittedly a number of passages which could be interpreted to give an Arian sense: Luke 2:52 spoke of Jesus growing in wisdom and stature. Hebrews 5:8 and 9 spoke of his learning obedience. John 12:27 and 28 said Christ's heart was troubled. John 14:28 said "... the Father is greater than I." In Matthew 26:39, Christ was said to submit his will to his Father's. In Mark 13:32, he said he did not know the time of his return, but that the Father did. In Proverbs 8, wisdom was "created" as the beginning of God's ways. In Acts 2:36, Jesus was made both Lord and Christ. In Hebrews 1:4, he was said to be greater than angels, but that he had "inherited" a name superior to theirs. In Colossians 1:15, he is called the "firstborn" of all creation.

In 1 Corinthians 15:28, it speaks of the Son being, in the end, subjected under God.

Arius had a way to deal with the fact that the Scriptures call the Son "God," too. Arius argued concerning John 1:1 that since θεός in the last phrase did not have the definite article, the Word was therefore not "the God," but simply "God," in some lesser sense. Fortunately for the orthodox, ὁ θεός (the God) was used of Christ at least in John 20:28 and Hebrews 1:8. The absence of the definite pronoun implied that Christ was of the *nature* of God. If there had been a definite pronoun used, it would have meant that "the Word" was all there was of God.

The orthodox party answered these arguments by referring the passages about the Son's subordination to the Father, about his weaknesses, his growth, and his lack of knowledge, either to his human nature only, which surely is the case with most of the passages, or to his own voluntary κενώσις ("emptying") for the sake of the salvation of men. They pressed home the passages which clearly showed the deity of Christ (John 1:1; 5:18; 10:30; 20:28; Heb. 1:5-11). When confronted with a verse such as Proverbs 8:22, they would answer that what was intended was not to teach the bringing of the Word into existence, but rather his close communion with the Father. Furthermore, they reasoned, if the Word were the wisdom of God (1 Cor. 1:24), then to say that at one time the Word did not exist would be to say that God was once without his wisdom. This would involve a change in the nature of God, something the Arians agreed was impossible.

It was at the Council of Nicea that Athanasius showed his great mental vigor and the promise of becoming the leader of the Nicene party. Though the *homoousian* party began the Council decidedly outnumbered by the middle-of-the-road *homoeousians*, the intellectual leadership of Athanasius quickly gave them the upper hand in debate, and many of the middle party moved quickly to their side.

Athanasius and the orthodox leaders had to argue against two parties. Against the Arians he pressed three points especially:

> First, he argued that Arianism undermined the Christian doctrine of God by presupposing that the divine Triad is not eternal and by virtually reintroducing polytheism. Secondly, it made nonsense of the established liturgical customs of baptizing in the Son's name as well as the Father's, and of addressing prayers to the Son. Thirdly, and perhaps most importantly, it undermined the Christian idea of redemption in Christ, since only if the Mediator was Himself divine could man hope to re-establish fellowship with God.[4]

Athanasius' arguments were more scriptural, however, than dogmatic and philosophical. Yet he could use philosophical arguments powerfully to defend trinitarianism and refute Arianism. At some times it seemed to Athanasius that all that was required to refute Arianism was to state the position, expound the biblical position, and allow the argument to refute itself. But at other times the Nicenes took more care to use definite scriptural arguments against particular Arian points.

One chief concern of the controversy was the importance of Christ's deity to the doctrine of salvation. A being who is not God could not do a work which only God could do, and the Nicene Fathers considered salvation to be precisely that sort of work. Only God could save, because God is the one who condemned (Gen. 3).

The scriptural proofs for the deity of the Son were abundant, and the Nicene Fathers used them. They also used the dogmatic arguments, and followed the same procedure with the doctrine of the Holy Spirit. Schaff describes the Nicenes' biblical arguments for the deity of the Holy Spirit:

The exegetical proofs employed by the Nicene fathers for the deity of the Holy Ghost are chiefly the following. The Holy Ghost is nowhere in Scripture reckoned among creatures or angels, but is placed in God Himself, co-eternal with God, as that which searches the depths of Godhead (1 Cor. 2:11, 12). He fills the universe, and is everywhere present (Ps. 139:7), while creatures, even angels, are in definite places. He was active even in the creation (Gen. 1:3), and filled Moses and the prophets. From Him proceeds the divine work of regeneration and sanctification (John 3:5; Rom. 1:4; 8:11; 1 Cor. 6:11; Tit. 3:5-7; Eph. 3:16; 5:17, 19, etc.). He is the source of all gifts in the church (1 Cor. 12). He dwells in believers, like the Father and the Son, and makes them partakers of the divine life. Blasphemy against the Holy Spirit is the extreme sin, which cannot be forgiven (Matt. 12:31). Lying to the Holy Ghost is lying to God (Acts 5:3, 4). In the formula of baptism (Matt. 28:19), and likewise in the apostolic benediction (2 Cor. 13:13), the Holy Ghost is put on a level with the Father and the Son, and yet distinguished from both; He must therefore be truly divine, yet at the same time a self-conscious person. The Holy Ghost is the source of sanctification, and unites us with the divine life, and thus must Himself be divine. The divine trinity tolerates in itself nothing created and changeable. As the Son is begotten of the Father from eternity, so the Spirit proceeds from the Father through the Son.[5]

The third party at Nicea, the *homoeousians*, or semi-Arians, argued that the Son had, not the same nature as the Father, but a nature "like" the Father's. Most of the *homoeousians* intended this to state a belief which was in content the same as that taught by the orthodox. Some of them used it as a mild way of expressing their Arianism. Few of them appeared to realize the impossibility of their position, given their formulation. They could not hope to satisfy the orthodox Fathers with such a postulate, for the latter would interpret "like substance" as an affirmation of two deities, and hence would level the charge of ditheism. On the other hand, they could not hope to satisfy the Arians, because the Arians believed the Son was of a substance totally unlike the Father's.

The formulation of the *homoeousians* was bound to cause misinterpretation. First, their use of οὐσία was decidedly different from that of any other group. In their terminology *ousia* approximated the sense of "person." This would never do, partly because the word did not mean that, and never had, but also because neither of the other parties could accept such a usage. What did that leave to express the substance of deity in Greek? With ὑπόστασις commonly accepted as the word for "person," οὐσία had to fill the need. The formulation indeed caused great misunderstanding.

The final decision of the Council was to accept a modified form of the creed submitted by Eusebius of Caesarea. The main modifications were the addition of the word ὁμοούσιον to describe the relation of the Son to the Father, and the addition of the anathema at the end. The creed which was accepted at that time read as follows:

We believe in one GOD, the FATHER Almighty, Maker of all things visible and invisible. And in one Lord JESUS CHRIST, the Son of God, begotten of the Father [the only-begotten; that is, of the essence of the Father, God of God], Light of Light, very God of very God, begotten, not made, being of one substance (ὁμοούσιον) with the Father; by whom all things were made [both in heaven and on earth]; who for us men, and for our salvation, came down and was incarnate and was made man; he suffered, and the third day he rose again, ascended into heaven; from thence he shall come to judge the quick and the dead. And in the HOLY GHOST. [But those who say: 'There was a time when he was not;' and 'He was not before he was made;' and 'He was made out of nothing,' or 'He is of another substance,' or 'The Son of God is created,' or 'changeable,' or 'alterable'—they are condemned by the holy catholic and apostolic Church.][6]

The word, ὁμοούσιος, of course, was the main bone of contention in the new form of the creed. The Athanasians were delighted at its presence. There was no possible way the Arians could reinterpret it to fit their theology, and it was impossible for any Arian, without being dishonest, to sign the Nicene Creed. Ruthless as this may seem, it was the only reasonable policy the Nicenes could take. It was essential that it be known who was Arian and who was not, for many Arians had been hiding behind ambiguous terms and broad generalities which failed to show their true colors. Many of the *homoeousians*, on the other hand, when finally confronted with the decision, realized that they could sign the Nicene Creed, and that the obnoxious word, as it was carefully explained by the Athanasians, was

119

not so obnoxious after all. Rather, it expressed just what they believed.

The great leader of the *homoeousians*, Eusebius of Caesarea, signed the creed along with the major portion of his party. His actual opinions on the nature of the Son are difficult to discern. Some historians believe that Eusebius went into the Council leaning favorably toward the true Arian side, and that when Arius defended himself in person at the Council, and Alexander snubbed Eusebius' attempts to make peace, Eusebius moved farther toward it.

Perhaps the explanation of the "inconsistency" in Eusebius' doctrine is in the distinction between logical and temporal priority. Since he signed the Nicene Creed, with all its definite teaching of the eternity of the Son and his consubstantiality with the Father, it seems highly unlikely that he would knowingly have denied the eternity of the Word. It may be that he meant that, since the Father generated the Son, he is therefore "before" the Son in the logical sense, though not in the temporal sense.

At any rate, sign the creed he did, and wrote a rather careful explanation to his home church in Caesarea explaining his action and his interpretation of the shibboleth ὁμοούσιος:

> When these articles of faith were proposed, there seemed to be no ground of opposition: nay, our most pious emperor himself was the first to admit that they were perfectly correct, and that he himself had entertained the sentiments contained in them; exhorting all present to give them their assent, and subscribe to these very articles, thus agreeing in a unanimous profession of them, with the insertion, however, of that single word "*homoousios*" (consubstantial), an expression which

the emperor himself explained, as not indicating corporeal affections or properties; and consequently that the Son did not subsist from the Father either by division or abscission: for, said he, a nature which is immaterial and incorporeal cannot possibly be subject to any corporeal affection; hence our conception of such things can only be in divine and mysterious terms. Such was the philosophical view of the subject taken by our most wise and pious sovereign; and the bishops on account of the word *homoousios,* drew up this formula of faith. [He then quoted the received form of the Nicene Creed.] Now this declaration of faith being propounded by them, we did not neglect to investigate the distinct sense of the expressions "of the substance of the Father, and consubstantial with the Father." Whereupon questions were put forth and answers, and the meaning of these terms was clearly defined; when it was generally admitted that *ousias* (of the essence of substance) simply implied that the Son is of the Father indeed, but does not subsist as a part of the Father. To this interpretation of the sacred doctrine which declares that the Son is of the Father, but is not a part of his substance, it seemed right to us to assent. We ourselves therefore concurred in this exposition; nor do we cavil at the word *"homoousios"* having regard to peace, and fearing to lose a right understanding of the matter. On the same grounds we admitted also the expression "begotten, not made": "for *made,"* said they, "is a term applicable in common to all the creatures which were made by the Son, to whom the Son has no resemblance. Consequently he is no creature like those which were made by him, but is of a substance far excelling any creature; which substance the Divine Oracles teach was begotten of the Father by such a mode of generation as cannot be explained nor even conceived by any creature." Thus also the declaration that "the Son is consubstantial with the Father" having been discussed, it was agreed that this must not be understood in a corporeal sense, or in any way analogous to mortal creatures; inasmuch as it is neither by division of substance, nor by abscission, nor by any change of the Father's substance and power, since the underived nature of the Father is inconsistent with these things. That he is consubstantial with the Father then simply implies, that the Son of God has no resemblance to created things, but is in every respect like the Father only who begat him; and that he is of no other substance or essence but of the Father.[7]

We have quoted Eusebius at length to avoid misunderstanding what he says. There seems no reason to think that he did not believe substantially what the Athanasian party believed, and that he simply preferred other terms to express the same thing. When he wrote that the Son is not to be thought a "part of the Father" or a "part of his substance," he was not denying the doctrine meant by ὁμοούσιος, but was avoiding a tripartite understanding of the term, the idea that the Father has part of the substance of deity, the Son part, and the Holy Spirit part, as if the substance of deity were "corporeal" and hence divisible. Instead deity is incorporeal and indivisible, from which it follows that none of the persons has a "part of" the substance, but each has that full substance.

If Eusebius was representative of most of the *homoeousians*, which he surely was, then we are certainly correct in judging that the *homoeousians* were actually in agreement with the *homoousians*, and that their signing of the Nicene Creed in no way compromised their honesty or implied that the creed did not truly succeed in stating the position of the orthodox in unambiguous terms. The fact that several decades later the vast majority of the *homoeousians* joined the Athanasian party is further evidence of this.

There was a fourth party at Nicea different in name only from the Arians: the Anomoeans. Their shibboleth was the word ἀνόμοιος, which meant "unlike." They believed the Son to be completely unlike the Father in substance. The fundamental point of their belief was identical with that of Arius. However, they did have some minor differences.

The Anomoeans played little part in the proceedings at Nicea, and it quickly became evident after the Council that their position was at least as bad as that of Arianism, if not worse, since it robbed the Godhead of all real attributes. It ended up with a God that was irrelevant to man, to the Son of God, and to "Itself," since there was nothing about it to be known, related to, or understood. It would be impossible for that God to reveal to men "its" will, for as it was so utterly simple it had no will. Anomoeanism was actually further from Christianity than Arianism had ever been, for it was not even, in its full logical implications, real theism. Of course, most of the Anomoeans themselves did not realize these implications. The orthodox quickly condemned the position. In this, for once, the Arians were in agreement with the orthodox, as were the semi-Arians.

The Creed had been set forth. The issues were out in the open, and the majority of the delegates to the Council were strongly in favor of it. The vast majority of the delegates signed it. Only five who were still at the Council by the time the Nicene Creed was presented for signatures would not sign: Eusebius of Nicomedia, the defender of Arianism; Theognis of Nice; Maris of Chalcedon; Theonas of Marmarica; and Secundus of Ptolemais. All objected for the same basic voiced reason: they understood ὁμοούσιος to teach the corporeality and divisibility of the Godhead. Most of them were also Arians.

Although the Council of Nicea ended with a rousing paper victory for the orthodox, the victory was not to be complete until fifty-six years later, at the Council of Constantinople. Shortly after the Council of Nicea, the Arians made a powerful comeback, taking the reins of power in the Church, at least in the East. They also gained the good favor of the Emperor Constantine and his son Constantius, who became emperor upon Constantine's death in 337, a year after the death of Arius. But even while the Arians were in power they were not completely unified.

ARIAN ASCENDANCY, A.D. 325-361

The Arian triumph after Nicea was won by two means in particular. First, the Arian party, knowing that it had been officially rejected by the majority of the Church realized that to gain the upper hand in the battle, they needed to turn to sources of power outside the ecclesiastical system. This meant turning to the emperor, for which they were well equipped, since Eusebius of Nicomedia, a leader of the Arians, had close ties with the emperor and his family. But the emperor wanted to believe what the holy catholic and apostolic Church believed. He had been convinced at Nicea that the Church believed the *homoousian*, orthodox position. Thus the Arians had to convince the emperor otherwise. This could not be done directly, since the emperor, though limited in theological understanding, had understood enough at Nicea to know the difference between ὁμοούσιος and ἑτεροούσιος, between God and demigod, between Creator and creature. The Arians could not simply say to the emperor, "Constantine, we believe Christ is a created being, the first creation of the Father, who can be called 'God' because of his participation in the Father's glory and his work in redemption, but who is not really God." They needed to hide their real beliefs by using ambiguous statements of faith. This is precisely what they did, and by this they gained the emperor's favor, appealing to him almost as if they were the poor, persecuted minority, and the mean Athanasians, who were really the culprits, were unjustly criticizing them of a mere misunderstanding and difference in words.

The forty years immediately following the Council of Nicea were some of the darkest hours for the orthodox faith. In other ways, however, those years proved the great strengthening ground for the Nicene formula and faith, and resulted in blessings. Almost immediately after the Council of Nicea the Arians turned to political means to gain power.

> This was a period of the greatest excitement in Church and State: Council was held against council; creed was set up against creed; anathema was hurled against anathema. "The highways," says the impartial heathen historian Ammianus Marcellinus, "were covered with galloping bishops." The churches, the theatres, the hippodromes, the feasts, the markets, the streets, the baths, and the shops of Constantinople and other large cities were filled with dogmatic disputes. In intolerance and violence the Arians even exceeded the orthodox. The interference of emperors and their courts only poured oil on the flames, and heightened the bitterness of contest by adding confiscation and exile to the spiritual punishment of synodical excommunication.[8]

125

While the primary theological defense of Arianism was carried on by Eusebius of Nicomedia, the ecclesiastical historian Eusebius of Caesarea, who was quite a diplomat, sought first the peace of the whole Church, regardless of theological differences. It was by his diplomacy, combined with an ambiguous confession of faith sent by Arius and Euzoius to Constantine, that Constantine was won to the side of the Arians, and later received Eusebius of Nicomedia into his close confidence, being baptized by him on his deathbed. When Constantine turned his favor to the Arians, he recalled Arius from exile, sent him again to Alexandria, and the Arians were back in power. It was at Constantine's insistence that Eusebius of Nicomedia became the Bishop of Constantinople the year after Constantine's death (A.D. 337), a position which Eusebius held from his consecration (A.D. 338) until Macedonius, another Arian, took possession of the see in 342 or 343.

The letter of Arius and Euzoius to Constantine is a study in ambiguity. The strictly theological portion, like Arius' "creed" of 328, was heretical, not so much for what it said as for what it failed to say. Constantine, unfortunately, apparently did not realize this, and by the time he knew what had happened he had already committed himself to the Arian party. Arius and Euzoius wrote:

> We believe in one God, the Father Almighty, and in His Son the Lord Jesus Christ, who was begotten from Him before all ages, God the Word, by whom all things were made, whether things in heaven or things on earth; He came and took upon Him flesh, suffered and rose again, and ascended into heaven, whence He will again come to judge the quick and the dead. We believe in the Holy Ghost, in the resurrection of the body, in the life to come, in the kingdom of heaven, and in one Catholic

Church of God, established throughout the earth. We have received this faith from the Holy Gospels, in which the Lord says to His disciples, 'Go forth and teach all nations, baptizing them in the name of the Father, and of the Son, and the Holy Ghost,' as they are taught by the whole Catholic Church and by the sacred Scriptures, as we believe in every point, let God be our judge, both now and in the day which is to come.[9]

Nothing in the statement expresses the Arian belief that Christ was a created being and not true God, but neither was there anything which denied such a belief. In addition, the appeal to the universality of the Church in such strong terms was clearly designed to focus the attention of the emperor on the unity of the Church rather than on the issue in question, namely, what sort of God the Church worships. The Arians, realizing that they could not win in ecclesiastical circles by open discussion and proclamation of beliefs, turned to politics and unity and harmony as more important than truth. Had they really believed in the supreme importance of truth, it seems that they would not have hidden the disunity in the Church. They would rather have tried, as did the Athanasians, to be sure all issues were out in the open where they could be discussed candidly and the truth determined.

Constantine, at any rate, was won to the side of the Arians, and protected them and their cause. Athanasius, who had become Bishop of Alexandria at Alexander's death (A.D. 326), was ordered to receive Arius back into fellowship after his banishment by the Council of Nicea to Illyria. In A.D. 330 Eustathius, one of the Nicene leaders, was overthrown from his bishopric in Antioch and replaced by Arian leadership. In the same year Eudoxius, an Arian, became Bishop of Germanicia. The Arians were moving rapidly into all the most important positions in the Church, aided constantly by imperial authority and persecution against the orthodox. At the insistence of Arian leadership, Constantine banished Athanasius to Gaul in 335. In 336, Arius was about to be received into fellowship in the Church at Constantinople when he died on his way to the communion service. The Arians claimed that he was poisoned; the orthodox thought it was an act of divine judgment.

Constantine died in 337 (May 22), having been baptized an Arian. Athanasius returned to Alexandria and the see, but was to remain there for only a short time. The following year Eusebius of Nicomedia became the Bishop of Constantinople, with Macedonius his chief presbyter. The Arians thus controlled all the most important sees in the Church, excluding Rome and Alexandria. In 339, however, Athanasius was banished again from Alexandria while Constantius, the son of Constantine, was emperor of the eastern half of the empire, and supported the Arians with every possible means, including imperial force. Athanasius went to Rome, where he was gladly received by Julius, the Bishop of Rome and a firm adherent of the Nicene orthodoxy. He continued on to Gaul, where he stayed with Hosius.

It was not until 346 that Athanasius was able to return to Alexandria. Ten years later he was attacked during a church service by Arians, who had with them Roman troops. Athanasius escaped from the city, and spent the next six years in exile, staying mostly with monks in the territory surrounding Alexandria. In 362, following the important Council of Alexandria, Athanasius was able to return to Alexandria, but after only a few months was banished yet again by Arian forces, with the assistance of the state. When Jovian became emperor, however, he terminated this exile, and Athanasius was back in Alexandria in 364. Jovian died, how-

ever, in October or November of that year, and less
than a year later the Arianizing emperor Valens banished him again. However, Valens was more a politi-
cian than a religious man, and when it became expe-
dient to do so, he returned Athanasius to the see in
366. Athanasius remained there until his death in 373,
at which time the "Three Cappadocians," Basil (the
Great) of Ancyra, Gregory of Nyssa, and Gregory of
Nazianzus became the prime defenders of the Nicene
faith.

Throughout this time Athanasius was writing vo-
luminously against the Arian heresy and others, including the "pneumatomachians," literally, "those
who fight against the Spirit," who accepted the deity
of Christ but called the Spirit an impersonal force.

With the death of Constantine, Constantius became
ruler of the East. He was completely in favor of the
Arians, and placed the power of the emperor behind
them in everything they did. Orthodoxy received se-
vere blows in the East and became the decided minority
among Church leadership, though it remained strong
in the West under the protection of the Emperor Constans. Constans died, however, in 350, and Constantius
became sole emperor. He did all he could to crush Nicene orthodoxy throughout the empire.

> The genuinely Arian elements in the great anti-
> Nicene party now threw off the mask and suc-
> ceeded in getting an unadulterated version of their
> teaching canonized at a series of synods, notably
> the third council of Sirmium (357) and the synods
> of Nicé (359) and Constantinople (360).[10]

The division of the Church along lines approximat-
ing the East/West halves of the empire was a situation
which neither the Church nor the empire could long
tolerate.

To heal this division, the two emperors, Constantius in the East and Constans in the West, summoned a general council at Sardica in Illyria, A.D. 343. Here the Nicene party and the Roman influence prevailed. . . . But the Arianizing Oriental bishops, dissatisfied with the admission of Athanasius, took no part in the proceedings, held an opposition council in the neighboring city of Philippopolis, and confirmed the decrees of the council of Antioch. The opposite councils, therefore, inflamed the discord of the church, instead of allaying it.[11]

The Council of Antioch had, in 341, decided upon a creed which opted for three hypostases united in one will. This was neither Arian nor orthodox, for it could be interpreted pleasingly by either side. The Arians at Philippopolis simply gave it an Arian interpretation and confirmed that. Constantius continued to favor strongly the Arians. It was clear that the Arians could never win in a truly representative council of all parts of the Church, as had been shown first at Nicea and later at Sardica. They therefore resorted to holding their own councils in opposition to the councils held by the orthodox and the "middle party," which was orthodox in theory but not in vocabulary.

Constantius' support of the Arians was not without difficulty, however. In 346 Constans put pressure on him which forced him to readmit Athanasius to the see of Alexandria. The death of Constans in 350, however, removed all restraints.

. . . after the death of Constans, A.D. 350, he [Constantius] summoned three synods in favor of a moderate Arianism; one at Sirmium in Pannonia (351), one at Arelate or Arels in Gaul (353), and one at Milan.in Italy (355); he forced the decrees of these councils on the Western church, deposed and banished bishops, like Liberius of Rome, Hosius of Cordova, Hilary of Poicters, Lucifer of Calaris, who resisted them, and drove Athanasius from the cathedral of Alexandria during divine service with five thousand armed soldiers, and supplied his place with an uneducated and avaricious Arian, George of Cappadocia (356). In these violent measures the court bishops and Eusebia, the last wife of Constantius and a zealous Arian, had great influence. Even in their exile the faithful adherents of the Nicene faith were subjected to all manner of abuse and vexation.[12]

Having gained the backing of the highest political power in the empire, the true Arians came completely into the open. Although this caused a great weakening of their position within the Church, for their decidedly anti-Christian view of Christ became clear, it also brought heightened power in the empire. As extreme as it may sound, Philip Schaff's summation of the Arian movement is probably correct:

Arianism was a religious political war against the spirit of the Christian revelation by the spirit of the world, which, after having persecuted the church three hundred years from without, sought under the Christian name to reduce her by degrading Christ to the category of the temporal and the created, and Christianity to the level of natural religion.[13]

The Arian party knew that it did not really represent either the contemporary Church or the centuries of the Church which preceded it. The claim by Arius and Euzoius in their letter to Constantine to be in step with Christianity was clearly false. They were quickly recognized by the Church itself as anything but Christian. Yet for some time, the Arian party was actually in titular and forceful control over the Church throughout the empire, even if not in spiritual and intellectual control.

But during this long reign of Arianism, orthodoxy and *homoeousianism* were not dormant and were far from silent. They, too, held their councils, wrote their letters and books, and proclaimed decrees and exiles of Arians. The giant among the defenders of orthodoxy, and clearly the leading thinker of the time in any party, was the great theologian Athanasius. It is to his dedication and toil that orthodoxy owes a great debt for the preservation of Nicene trinitarianism, and therefore also of biblical trinitarianism, in the fourth century and beyond.

The Athanasians and the *homoeousians* were actually in agreement in what they believed concerning the Godhead. Both parties realized it was impossible that the Godhead should contain anything created, and both sides realized that Father, Son, and Holy Spirit were all proclaimed in Scripture as members of the Godhead.

For Athanasius and the orthodox, the equal deity of Father, Son, and Holy Spirit was essential to both the fact and the sense of redemption according to the gospel. The purpose of redemption is the uniting of men with God in a perfect bond, and none other than God can accomplish this. Athanasius brought this out especially in speaking of the Son's work in redemption:

> And this has been done, since the own Word of God Himself, who is from the Father, has put on the flesh, and become man. For if, being a creature, He had become man, man had remained just what he was, not joined to God; for how had a work been joined to the Creator by a work? or (sic) what

succour had come from like to like, when one as well as other needed it? And how, were the Word a creature, had He power to undo God's sentence, and to remit sin, whereas it is written in the Prophets, that this is God's doing? For "who is a God like unto Thee, that pardoneth iniquity, and passeth by transgression?" For whereas God has said, "Dust thou art, and unto dust shalt thou return," men have become mortal; how then could things originate undo sin? but (sic) the Lord is He who has undone it, as He says Himself, "Unless the Son shall make you free;" and the Son, who made free, has shewn in truth that He is no creature, nor one of things originate, but the proper Word and Image of the Father's Essence, who at the beginning sentenced, and alone remitteth sins.[14]

In addition to the possibility of redemption by a creature, Athanasius saw that if Christ were a mere creature, the battle against evil could never be decisively won by him, for the devil also is a creature, and final victory could not be had by one creature over another.

The real task for orthodoxy and the great middle party was to hammer out a formulation of the doctrine which was verbally acceptable to all. This involved the dispute over ὁμοούσιος and ὁμοιούσιος, and οὐσία and ὑπόστασις. The Athanasians used the latter two words as synonyms, meaning "substance" or "nature," while the *homoeousians* used ὑπόστασις for "person" and ουσία for substance. In his *Statement of Faith*, 1, Athanasius wrote, "Neither can we imagine three Subsistences [τρεῖς ὑποστάσεις] separated from each other, as results from their bodily nature in the case of men, lest we hold a plurality of gods like the heathen."[15]

A council at Antioch (A.D. 344) attempted to avoid such difficult terms and state the orthodox faith in more simple language. The creed which it produced,

133

called the *Ecthesis Macrostichos* ("Long-lined Creed") was a good attempt at this:

> It scrupulously avoids contentious terms like *ousia* and *hypostasis*, and rejects the idea of the Son's generation out of nothingness, as also the formula 'There was when He was not'. The Son, it declares, is 'from God alone'. The Father alone is 'ingenerate' and 'unoriginate', and He begets the Son 'outside time'. The Son is 'perfect and true God in nature'; His coming to be (ὕπαρξις) is 'before the ages'. The Three are 'three objects and three Persons' (πράγματα . . . πρόσωπα: the latter word is no doubt chosen as translating the Western *persona*), but Their inseparability is forcefully emphasized. 'They are united with each other without mediation or distance', and possess 'one dignity of Godhead'.[16]

It was mediatory attempts such as this which gradually brought the orthodox and the *homoeousians* together, for in these councils they saw more and more the substantial unity of their beliefs. Eleven years later the unity of the two parties became clear:

> In 359, a Homoeousian memorandum was drafted which reveals how rapidly the gap between the new party and the Nicenes was narrowing. First, after explaining that Eastern theologians simply used ὑπόστασις to express 'the subsistent characteristics of the Persons', this lays it down that Father and Son are two hypostases, and that from this point of view 'a likeness in respect of substance' (κατ' οὐσίαν ὁμοιότης) exists between Them. But, secondly, it adds that the Son, having been begotten from the Father, is spirit like Him, and from this point of view is 'one and the same'

(τὸ αὐτό) as He. Although the identity here presupposed is qualitative rather than numerical, the memorandum clearly marks an approximation to the Athanasian point of view.[17]

The qualitative identity of Father and Son, for the eastern theologians, was the same as saying that they were the same God, for to them only God has the true qualities of the Father.

Athanasius and other representatives of orthodoxy met time and again with the *homoeousians* to discuss their differences in vocabulary, and they finally worked it out that the easterners were welcome to speak of three hypostases so long as what they meant by that was three persons, not three essences or substances; and they could speak of three persons "like" in substance, so long as what they meant was that the persons were the same God, and were only attempting to avoid Sabellianism in not saying "same in substance." Meanwhile, the easterners gave the westerners leave to speak of one hypostasis, so long as they were using it as synonymous with οὐσία and not intending to teach Sabellianism. Thus Athanasius could speak, using the eastern meaning of the word, of three hypostases, or he could speak of one, using the western meaning.

At the same time he bore in mind that the three hypostases in God were not to be regarded as separated in any way, since this would lead to polytheism. According to him the unity of God as well as the distinctions in His Being are best expressed in the term 'oneness of essence'. This clearly and unequivocally expresses the idea that the Son is of the same substance as the Father, but also implies that the two may differ in other respects, as, for instance, in personal subsistence.[18]

While the orthodox and the *homoeousian* parties, then, were coming closer and closer together, the Arian party and the Arian elements within the *homoeousian* party were splitting into ever smaller groups, and hence lost their strength and influence in the Church. The Arian domination became one purely of politics, not of actual spirit or form of the faith. The backing of Constantius encouraged the Arians to come into the open more and more, and "... as a result of the very triumph of extremism, the moderates in the vast amorphous party began to rally under Basil of Ancyra around the compromise formula 'of like substance' (ὁμοιούσιος)." That vast amorphous party, of course, was the middle party, and its adoption of the *homoeousian* formula spelled the end of Arianism as a driving force in the Church. It was inevitable that the later union of the true *homoeousians* and the orthodox should occur, and that the Arians who had adopted the *homoeousian* formula for the sake of ease should be forced to admit their disagreement with the real meaning of ὁμοιούσιος. As things stood, there were three parties which really stood for only two positions: orthodoxy and Arianism. Within the Arian party there were factions, however, which weakened it, and they spread further and further apart. The factions within orthodoxy, however, moved closer together, until they finally presented a unified front against the Arians. This is how things stood on the eve of the important Council of Alexandria, A.D. 362.

UNION OF ORTHODOXY AND THE FINAL VICTORY (A.D. 362-381)

The last phase of the Arian controversy, stretching from the apparent triumph of Arianism under Constantius, through the Council of Alexandria which spelled the death of Arianism, and finally to the Council of Constantinople, A.D. 381, brought the disintegration of Arianism from within. It brought also its destruction, intellectually and morally, from without—and the triumph of orthodoxy in the ratification of an expanded form of the Nicene Creed. And it resulted in the imperial enforcement of that creed by the emperor Theodosius I, who ascended to the throne in 379 and reigned through 395. The temporarily dominant *homoeousian* party grew quickly closer to the *homoousians*, until at last they became a united power against Arianism in all its forms. The parties finally united when they overcame their disagreement about the uses of the term ὑπόστασις and οὐσία.

Athanasius twice in the *Tome to the Antiochenes* explains the difficulty with the words, and the temporary settlement which the Alexandrine council worked out. First he describes the eastern position as he understood it after the easterns had explained their ideas about the terms:

> For as to those whom some were blaming for speaking of three Subsistences (ὑποστάσειζ), on the ground that the phrase is unscriptural and therefore suspicious, we thought it right indeed to require nothing beyond the confession of Nicæa, but on account of the contention we made enquiry of them, whether they meant, like the Arian madmen, subsistences foreign and strange, and alien in essence from one another, and that each Subsistence was divided apart by itself, as is the case with creatures in general and in particular with those begotten of men, or like different substances, such as gold, silver, or brass;—or whether, like other heretics, they meant three Beginnings and three Gods, by speaking of three Subsistences.
>
> They assured us in reply that they neither meant this nor had ever held it. But upon our asking them

'what then do you mean by it, or why do you use such expressions?' they replied, Because they believed in a Holy Trinity, not a trinity in name only, but existing and subsisting in truth, 'both a Father truly existing and subsisting, and a Son truly substantial and subsisting, and a Holy Spirit subsisting and really existing do we acknowledge,' and that neither had they said there were three Gods or three beginnings, nor would they at all tolerate such as said or held so, but that they acknowledged a Holy Trinity but One Godhead, and one Beginning, and that the Son is coessential with the Father, as the fathers said; while the Holy Spirit is not a creature, nor external, but proper to and inseparable from the Essence of the Father and the Son.

He then explains the western (or old eastern) way of expressing belief in the Trinity, namely, three πρόσωπα in one ὑπόστασις (using the latter as equivalent to οὐσία), which had been misinterpreted by many of the delegates at the conference as Sabellianism:

But they in their turn assured us that they neither meant this nor had ever held it, but 'we use the word Subsistence thinking it the same thing to say Subsistence or Essence;' 'But we hold that there is One, because the Son is of the Essence of the Father, and because of the identity of nature. For we believe that there is one Godhead, and that it has one nature, and not that there is one nature of the Father, from which that of the Son and of the Holy Spirit are distinct.' Well, thereupon they who had been blamed for saying there were three Subsistences agreed with the others, while those who had spoken of One Essence, also confessed the doctrine of the former as interpreted by them.

138

And by both sides Arius was anathematised as an adversary of Christ, and Sabellius, and Paul of Samosata, as impious men, and Valentinus and Basilides as aliens from the truth, and Manichæus as an inventor of mischief.[19]

After three centuries of development, the language of trinitarianism finally looked as if it were going to reach a consensus as these terms were worked out. As it turned out, the consensus was reached, except for some fringe groups, only nineteen years later at Constantinople. Most important was that it was recognized by both parties that language itself was not of paramount importance, but what the language meant. And with this agreement, they were able to see that each side meant the same thing while saying it in different ways.

The two parts of the orthodox party now formed a bond against Arianism which assured the latter's destruction. There was no longer any real "middle party" between the orthodox and the Arians. Those who were still called "semi-Arians" were definitely not orthodox. Some of them accepted the true consubstantiality of Father and Son, but called the Spirit either a created being or the impersonal power of God. Most clung to the *homoeousian* formula in a futile attempt to hide their real Arianism. The spiritual victory of orthodoxy was complete by A.D. 362. The next nineteen years were spent winning the outward victory, removing Arianism from ecclesiastical and political power.

The task was not easy. The Emperor Valens (reigned 364-378) was a fanatical Arian and heavily persecuted the orthodox party. He forced bishops into exile and handed over their sees to Arians, used physical torment against some, and attempted to make Arianism the final victor in ecclesiastical circles. It became increasingly difficult for the orthodox to worship openly.

When Gregory of Nazianzus was called to Constantinople in 379, there was but one small congregation in the city which had not become Arian; but his able and eloquent sermons on the deity of Christ, which won him the title "the Theologian," contributed powerfully to the resurrection of the catholic faith.[20]

Arianism continued to decline in spiritual, intellectual, and moral strength, and with that decline came a loss of support among the common members of the Church. The support of the emperor, great and powerful as it was, could not hope to counterbalance the weight of the decisions of the Church as a body. During the reign of Gratian, the successor to Valens, the orthodox party made great gains in winning back sees, for Gratian was completely disinterested in ecclesiastical affairs, and the Church was free to govern her own life. By now "the Church" had come to be almost synonymous with the orthodox party, for the majority of members agreed with them against the Arian leadership.

Thus the heretical party was already in reality intellectually and morally broken, when the emperor Theodosius I ... a Spaniard by birth, and educated in the Nicene faith, ascended the throne, and in his long and powerful reign (379-395) externally completed the triumph of orthodoxy in the Roman empire. Soon after his accession he issued, in 380, the celebrated edict, in which he required all his subjects to confess the orthodox faith, and threatened the heretics with punishment.[21]

The orthodox bishops and the emperor called the Council at Constantinople, which met in 381, to make

140

final and official the triumph of the Nicene faith. The main purpose of the council was simply to ratify the Nicene Creed and recognize its place as the confession of the Catholic Church. Constantinople thus marked the final and complete victory of orthodoxy over Arianism in the Church within the Roman Empire and, for the most part, outside it as well.

The Council of Constantinople not only marked the victory of orthodoxy over heresy, but also pronounced the independence of the Church from the state. At first glance it might appear that the only reason orthodoxy finally won is that Emperor Theodosius I was orthodox. But this is not really the case. The Church had conquered the throne, not vice versa. The constant characteristic of Arianism from beginning to end was dependence on imperial might for protection and power.

> Arianism associated itself with the secular political power and the court party; it represented the imperi-papal principle, and the time of its prevalence under Constantius was an uninterrupted season of the most arbitrary and violent encroachments of the state upon the rights of the church. Athanasius, on the contrary, who was so often deposed by the emperor, and who uttered himself so boldly respecting Constantius, is the personal representative not only of orthodoxy, but also of the independence of the church with reference to the secular power, and in this respect a precursor of Gregory VII in his contest with the German imperialism.[22]

The inherent independence of orthodoxy from the state is implied in its doctrines of God and redemption: Because redemption is the work whereby God himself atones for man's sins, frees him from bondage to sin, and unites him with God, the redeemed Church and the redeemed individual have finally a higher authority than the state. While the Christian is to submit himself to the state (Romans 13), he and the Church must together repeat, at every attempt of the state to encroach on the rights of the Church, "We must obey God rather than men!" (Acts 5:29). The Arian concept of God and redemption could not result in such an attitude. It was not God who was said to redeem, but a fellow creature like ourselves; and hence it was not really to God that we were united, but to another creature. Under this thinking, the Church and the individual Christian would have an authority only as high as any creature can have over another. This would not give them the authority of God.

It was not by the power of the empire that orthodoxy won. Had Theodosius not been a Nicene, Arianism would have died under the weight of the orthodox arguments anyway. Orthodoxy had defeated heresies in the past without the help of the emperor, and in time it surely would have defeated this foe as well.

The Nicene-Constantinopolitan Creed comes at the end of three-and-a-half centuries of battle against gnosticism, neo-platonism, subordinationism, polytheism, Monarchianism, and finally Arianism, each with many forms. It expresses the faith taught in the New Testament as contrasted with all the variations offered by the unorthodox in the past who failed to represent that faith accurately. The Nicene Creed stands as the great hallmark of truly Christian trinitarianism against all pseudo-Christian trinities.

IV

THE NICENE CREED AND THE NEW TESTAMENT DOCTRINE OF THE TRINITY

W E have traced the development of trinitarianism from the New Testament through more than three centuries of the early Church. We have stressed along the way the continuity which we have witnessed in concept, even while there is difference in vocabulary.

Three steps are necessary to show that the Nicene-Constantinopolitan Creed is an accurate representation of the New Testament doctrine of the Trinity. We must see what the Nicene Creed itself means, not just what the words are, but what they meant to those who wrote it. We must also compare what the New Testament says, as we have discovered in chapter one. We must see if the two agree with each other.

We must not contend that the Nicene Creed *looks like* the New Testament. The creed is an exercise in systematic theology. Although there are portions of the New Testament which are highly theological, the one thing we cannot say is that any of it is systematic theology as it was practiced three hundred years later.

Since we have quoted in full the Nicene Creed in the first chapter and again in the second, we will not reproduce it all here, but will look only at those portions which directly pertain to the doctrine of the Trinity.

The first article of the creed concerns the belief in monotheism and the person of the Father:

> I believe in one GOD THE FATHER Almighty; Maker of heaven and earth, and of all things visible and invisible.

The person and nature of the Father were never in doubt in the early Church except among the clearly anti-Christian Marcionites. The Father was constantly recognized as the true God of the Judeo-Christian religious system, and the creeds of the early Church never contradicted this belief. The great significance in this first article is not so much that the Father is called God as that the Nicene Creed begins by affirming the belief in *one* God. One of the Arian arguments against the doctrine of the Trinity was that it led inevitably to tritheism. This the Nicene Fathers and their followers at Constantinople wished to answer from the first.

It is significant also how the Father is described. He is the "maker of heaven and earth, and of all things visible and invisible." The same is later attributed to the Son, "by Whom all things were made." If it is once established that the Creator of all things is God, then if it is later established that any person is the Creator of all things, then it is established that that person is God: for how could the Creator of all things be himself created? And only if he is created is he not God, for God alone is uncreated.

The first article of the Nicene Creed, then, teaches that there is a Person called the Father, and that he is the one Almighty God. It describes God as the Creator of heaven and earth, and of all things visible and invisible.

The second article contains the teaching concerning the nature and redemptive work of Christ, the Son. We quote here only that which pertains to his nature:

> And in one Lord JESUS CHRIST, the only-begotten Son of God, begotten of the Father before all worlds [God] of God, Light of Light, very God of very God, begotten, not made, being of one substance [essence] with the Father; by whom all things were made; . . . was incarnate by the Holy Ghost. . .and was made man. . . .

This second article bears the primary weight of the trinitarian teaching of the Nicene Creed. The first article states something uncontested; the third applies to the Spirit the same glory and worship which is due to the Father and the Son. If the Son's nature is such that he is to be worshiped as the true God, then so also must be the Spirit's nature. It is in this second article, then, that the authors did the major work of stating and supporting the doctrine of the Trinity.

The parallel formation of the creed is not to be passed by without mention. The three great points are: I believe . . . in the Father; and . . . in the Son; and . . . in the Holy Spirit. All other material which does not deal specifically with the identity of the Father, Son, and Spirit comes in the form of subpoints. There is then from the very formation of the creed a special emphasis placed on the equal adoration of the three persons.

We begin with the fact that Jesus Christ is "Lord." The New Testament uses the word "lord" of people as well as of God. However, there is a technical use of the word in which it substitutes for YHWH (Jehovah, Yahweh) in the Old Testament, and it is clearly used in that sense occasionally in reference to Jesus (Phil. 2:11, 12; Heb. 1:8-12). It was a most emphatic way of

147

affirming belief in the absolute deity of Christ. Indeed, for Christians there is "one Lord," Jesus Christ (1 Cor. 8:6), and if God is to be Lord at all, and Jesus is the "one Lord," then Christ must be affirmed to be God. Had the Nicenes written of "two Lords, the Father and the Son," they would no doubt have destroyed all semblance of a doctrine of the Trinity, for they would have driven an immovable wedge between two beings, the Father and the Son, affirming them to be different Lords, and hence denying the very core of Christian revelation, which is that "Jesus Christ is Lord" (Phil. 2:11, 12; 1 Cor. 8:6; 12:1, 2).

Jesus Christ is called the "only-begotten Son of God." The use here of "begotten" was carefully selected (μονογενής, *unigenitum*), for it affirmed of the Son, not that he came into existence, but that his relation to the Father was one of "begetting," that is, of what was later called "filiation" (which simply means to be a son). The use of this word was scriptural (John 1:18; 3:16). It affirmed of the Son a unique relation with the Father, a relation which no other person in existence has. While all created things are "created," and while the Holy Spirit is not begotten but rather "proceeds" out from the Father, the Son is "begotten" of the Father. The whole Judeo-Christian concept of reproduction would lie behind this word, but in a modified sense.

Life reproduces after its own kind. If the son of man is man, the Son of God is God. But while the son of man is *a* man, the Son of God is not "a God," for there is only one God. Thus for one to be the Son of God means to have the very nature that God has. In addition, while the son of man is always temporally secondary to his father, the Son of God, being in very nature God, must be eternal, and hence is not temporally second. This fact stems not only from the fact

148

that he has the nature of God, but also from the fact that God himself is unchangeable, immutable (Rom. 1:19-21). If at any time the Son of God, being God, were to come into existence, there would be two changes in God: God would become a Father, whereas he was not before; and God would increase. But for an infinite being, increase is impossible; and for an unchangeable being, change is impossible. Therefore the Son must be . . .

"Begotten of the Father before all worlds [ages]." That is, his generation must be from eternity. There never was a time when he was not, for even before all ages he was the Son of God. The Word, the Son, therefore, is eternal (John 1:1-3; Heb. 13:8; John 8:58). And for the same reason he is . . .

"God of God, Light of Light, true God of true God," three phrases designed to reiterate and emphasize the same point. The deity of the Son is a true deity, not a derived or participatory deity. He is not "a God" in the sense which the Arians were willing to allow of him. As the Son of the true God, he must himself be the true God, for the same reason that the son of a true man must be truly a man. The repetitive nature of these phrases is evidenced by the fact that the Latin version of Dionysius Exiguus, quoted above, does not include the phrase "God of God," nor does the Greek, and the Received Text of the Roman Catholic Church includes it as a later recension. The original Nicene Creed, however, did include it. The Fathers saw that such repetition was unnecessary to their point; some wished to retain it (perhaps for aesthetic reasons?) as it provides a fitting rhythm to the text. It later became a wonderful theme on which the composers of the great masses could play. Others, hoping to streamline the creed and use only what was necessary to clarify the belief, left it out. It makes no difference, finally, to the meaning.

While the Arians could reinterpret "God of God" to fit their theology, they could not possibly do so with "true God of true God," and thus the Nicene Creed accomplished its task of stating something in terms so unambiguous that they could not be misunderstood or misinterpreted.

The Son, as the "Son" of God, was "begotten, not made." This was necessary to allay misunderstanding of the word "begotten"; for as was noted earlier, contemporary philosophical parlance had begun to use "beget" as a synonym for "bring into existence." The Greek and Latin texts, as well as the English, have woven this part of the text carefully into the pattern. God the Father is "Maker" of all things, but the Son is not "made." Thus the Son cannot possibly be numbered among the things which are "made" by the Father, as the Arians held. This again teaches the eternity of the Son (John 1:1-3; 8:58).

Not only is the Son not made, he is of the same substance with the Father. There is no doubt that the term *homoousius* is unscriptural. But the concept expressed by it is scriptural to the core: the Son is God (John 20:28), the true God (1 John 5:20), the Son of God (John 3:16), and as such he must have the nature of God. Indeed, the most thorough studies of John 1:1 have shown that the concept expressed there is that the Word has the very nature of God. The Word, then, is ὁμοούσιος, *consubstantial* with the Father. The language of Nicene orthodoxy is therefore scriptural in meaning in spite of the fact that it is not scriptural in term.

Being of the same nature or substance with the Father, the Son, too, is Creator. He is as truly the One "by whom all things were made" as is the Father. In this case not only is the thought scriptural, but the phrase itself is almost identical to Scripture (John 1:3; Col. 1:15-18).

150

So the Son of God is the same God whose Son he is: but he is not the same person whose Son he is. "I believe in one God the Father . . . *and* in one Lord Jesus Christ . . . begotten of the Father . . . one substance with the Father. . .sitteth on the right hand of the Father." The distinction between Father and Son as persons was clearly implied in the creed. By that time theological discussion normally expressed this either as τρεῖς ὑποστάσεις or *tria persona*, though neither phrase is used in the Nicene Creed. The fact that there was no explicit description of Father, Son, and Spirit as "three persons" is not materially important. It was commonly accepted by all that they were distinct from each other and that each was personal. There can be no modalism attached to this creed either.

In case there were any misunderstandings, the Nicene Creed added the fact that the Son "was incarnate by the Holy Ghost . . . and was made man." This divine Son of God is none other than the Jesus Christ who walked the earth, lived a perfect life, "was crucified also for us under Pontius Pilate; he suffered and was buried; and the third day he rose again . . . and ascended into heaven." There is no room for gnostic docetism here. The Son of God really became a man.

The Christ of the Nicene Creed is then both man and God. As the Son of God he is distinct from the Father personally, but is the same substance or essence with the Father. All of these things we saw in the New Testament. So also we saw in the New Testament that he is Creator of all things. He is "begotten, not made." The Christ of the Nicene Creed and the Father of the Nicene Creed are the same as are taught by the New Testament.

The third article teaches of the Holy Spirit:

And I believe in the Holy Ghost, the Lord and Giver of Life; who proceedeth from the Father [and

151

the Son]; who with the Father and the Son together is worshiped and glorified.

The Holy Spirit, with the Son, is "the Lord." This is no casual use of the word, as one might call a civil authority "lord," but is parallel to its use with the Son. He then who is Lord along with the Son is the same Lord, namely the "Lord" of the New Testament, the way of referring to Jehovah in the Old (2 Cor. 3:17; 1 Cor. 8:6; Phil. 2:11, cf. Isa. 45:23). As Lord, the Holy Spirit is God. He is not an impersonal force, for such a force could never be called "Lord."

The Holy Spirit also is the "Giver of life" (John 3:5; Rom. 8:10). This is his part in redemption, for the "life" thought of here is not the mere life of organic material, but the "life" eternal, of which Paul spoke: "Once I was alive apart from the law; but when the commandment came, sin sprang to life and I died" (Rom. 7:9, 10). He gave us the opposite of "death," which is the payment for sin (Rom. 6:23). Here the Fathers argued as they did concerning the Son. How can a creature have a part in redemption, in giving new life to sinful, dead men whose sentence of death came from God? If he does this, the Holy Spirit must not be a creature. As an eternal being, he certainly cannot be.

The Holy Spirit "proceedeth from the Father." The Fathers saw such a procession as an indication of the consubstantiality of the Spirit with the Father, and with the Son also, for as eternal he is not created (Heb. 9:14); if he is distinct personally from the Father (John 14:16), then his procession from the Father must be one of enduring in the same substance, for in eternity past there was no other substance but that of God in which the Spirit could subsist. The fact that in some sense he does "proceed" was clear to them from John 15:26: "who goes out from the Father." That this

152

procession is not a temporal thing they reasoned from the fact that he is eternal and that he is eternally distinct. He was active also in creation (Gen. 1:2; Job 33:4).

He also "with the Father and the Son together [is] glorified." There can be no higher position than this, for the Father and Son have been declared to be the true God, and to worship and glorify one along with them is thus to do so in recognition that he, too, is God. It is God only who is to be worshiped by the Christian (Luke 4:8), and he will not share his glory with another (Isa. 48:11-13). The exaltation of the Spirit to this position of receiving worship and glory due the Father and Son can be understood as nothing less than acknowledging him to be the very God who the Father and Son are.

He also is distinct from them in person. It is not ". . . that is, I believe in the Holy Ghost," but ". . . and in the Holy Ghost." It is not "who as the Father and the Son together is worshiped and glorified," but "who with the Father and the Son together is worshiped and glorified."

The Holy Spirit in the Nicene Creed, then, is God just as are the Father and the Son, and this is precisely what we found in the New Testament (2 Cor. 3:17; Acts 5:3, 4; Heb. 9:14). He is also distinct from them personally (John 14:26; 15:26; 16:7).

The Nicene Creed, then, with centuries of theological discussion and controversy behind it, still teaches of the Trinity as the New Testament does: that the Father, the Son, and the Holy Spirit, while distinct from each other personally, are the same God.

This is not only New Testament content, it is New Testament structure as well. We saw earlier the development of the creeds and confessions of faith through the centuries leading to Nicea and Constantinople, and that they developed along the lines laid down in the sending of the disciples, who were to "make disciples of all nations, baptizing them in the name of the Father and of the Son and of the Holy Spirit" (Matt. 28:19). The same construction occurs here. The confession is at heart just what is implied there. We are to believe in the Father, and in the Son, and in the Holy Spirit. These three phrases are the skeletal structure of the Nicene Creed: "I believe in one God the Father . . . and in one Lord Jesus Christ, the . . . Son . . . and in the Holy Ghost." All other material is explanation of what we believe about these persons.

The creed adopted at Constantinople did not retain substantially the same form as that adopted at Nicea fifty-six years earlier without a struggle in the interim. The main bone of contention continued to be the word ὁμοούσιος. However, all alternatives were found finally lacking in some way: "Exact image of the Godhead" (Second Creed of Antioch, A.D. 341) came close, but it still allowed for a substantial division between the Son and God. "Like the Father who begot Him according to the Scriptures" (Dated Creed, Fourth of Sirmium) allowed for subordination. "Like the Father in all things" (Dated Creed, Fourth of Sirmium) was better, but it was pointed out by the Nicenes that the difference between created and uncreated substance is absolute. Thus if the Son is uncreated, his substance is not only "like" the Father's, it is the same as the Father's; while if he is created, his substance is unlike the Father's. The same problem hampered the formula, "of like essence with the Father" (Ancyra, 358). "Unlike the Father" was clearly Arian in its implication, if not in its vocabulary.[1] The only sure solution was the use of ὁμοούσιος. It had long since been made clear that it did not imply Sabellianism, and by the time of Constantinople the support for it was nearly unanimous (especially since "one ὑπόστασις" could no longer pos-

154

sibly be accepted, it being the accepted custom to use that word for "person"). The contention was ended for all practical purposes by A.D. 381. The word clearly served a definite purpose, both positive and negative:

> At first it had a negative meaning against heresy; denying, as Athanasius repeatedly says, that the Son is in any sense created or produced and changeable. But afterwards the homoousian became a positive test-word for orthodoxy, designating, in the sense of the Nicene council, clearly and unequivocally, the vertiable (sic) and essential deity of Christ, in opposition to all sorts of apparent or half divinity, or mere similarity to God. The same divine, eternal, unchangeable essence, which is in an original way in the Father, is, from eternity, in a derived way, through generation, in the Son; just as the water of the fountain is in the stream, or the light of the sun is in the ray, and cannot be separated from it. . . . This is the sense of the expression: "God of God," "very God of very God." Christ, in His divine nature, is as fully consubstantial with the Father, as, in His human nature, He is with man. . . .[2]

It need not even be asked whether they meant "generic unity" or "numeric unity" when they used the term. Either would come to the same thing, for they believed the divine substance to be absolutely indivisible and hence one. Thus even if they only meant generic unity, they would have seen the fact that this implied numeric unity of substance as well.

CONCLUSION

The New Testament teaches us that there is one God and that this God is three distinct persons, the Father, the Son, and the Holy Spirit, and that these persons are co-equal and co-eternal. This is also the only possible interpretation of the Nicene Creed as it was intended by its authors. Therefore, the doctrine of the Trinity as taught in the Nicene Creed is an accurate representation of the teaching of the New Testament.

NOTES

INTRODUCTION

1. Adapted from Philip Schaff, *Creeds of Christendom* (Grand Rapids: Baker Book House, 1977), II:66-68.

CHAPTER ONE

1. In Alfred E. J. Rawlinson, ed., *Essays on the Trinity and the Incarnation* (London & N.Y.: Longmans, Green, 1928), p. 199.
2. Augustus Strong, *Systematic Theology* (Old Tappan, N.J.: Revell, 1976), p. 308.
3. *International Standard Bible Encyclopedia* (Grand Rapids: Eerdmans, 1956), s.v. "Trinity."
4. R.C. Trench, *Synonyms of the New Testament* (Grand Rapids: Eerdmans, 1976 rpt.), p. 262.
5. H. E. Dana and Julius R. Mantey, *A Manual Grammar of the Greek New Testament* (N.Y.: Macmillan, revised ed., 1957), p. 148.
6. See two of the most important studies recently: E. Cadman Colwell, "A Definite Rule for the Use of the Article in the Greek New Testament," *Journal of Biblical Literature* 52 (1933): 12-21; Philip B. Harner, "Qualitative Anarthrous Predicate Nouns; Mark 15:39 and John 1:1," *Journal of Biblical Literature* 92 (March 1973): 75-87.
7. A. T. Robertson, *Word Pictures in the New Testament* (Nashville: Broadman, 1934), Vol. 5, p. 4.
8. C. F. D. Moule, "The New Testament and the Doctrine of the

Trinity: A Short Report on an Old Theme," *Expository Times* 88 (Oct. 1976), p. 17.

9. James O. Buswell, Jr., *A Systematic Theology of the Christian Religion* (Grand Rapids: Zondervan, 1973), Vol. 1, pp. 110, 111.

10. Hendrikus Berkhof, *The Doctrine of the Holy Spirit* (Atlanta: John Knox Press, 1977).

11. C. F. D. Moule, "N.T. and Trinity," p. 18.

12. Cited in Moule, "N.T. and Trinity," p. 19

13. *International Standard Bible Encyclopedia*, s.v. "Trinity."

CHAPTER TWO

1. J. A. T. Robinson, *Redating the New Testament* (Philadelphia: Westminster, 1974), pp. 352, 353.

2. J. B. Lightfoot, ed., *The Apostolic Fathers* (Grand Rapids: Baker, 1976), p. 126.

3. Kelly, *Early Christian Doctrines*, p. 87.

4. Alexander Roberts and James Donaldson, eds., *The Ante-Nicene Fathers* (Grand Rapids: Eerdmans, 1975 rpt.), Vol. 1, p. 52, *Ephesians* 7.

5. Ibid., Vol. 1, p. 183.

6. Ibid., Vol. 1, p. 331.

7. Kelly, *Early Christian Doctrines*, p. 89.

8. A. Harnack, "Athenagoras," in *The New Schaff-Herzog Encyclopedia of Religious Knowledge* (Grand Rapids: Baker, 1977), Vol. 1, p. 347.

9. Roberts and Donaldson, *Ante-Nicene Fathers*, Vol. 2, p. 133, *A Plea for the Christians*, x.

10. Ibid., Vol. 2, p. 133.

11. Ibid., Vol. 2, pp. 100, 101, *Epistle to Autolycus*, II, xv.

12. Arthur C. McGiffert, *A History of Christian Thought* (New York: Charles Scribner's Sons, 1947) Vol. 2, p. 12, n. 1.

13. Roberts and Donaldson, *Ante-Nicene Fathers*, Vol. 3, p. 621, *Against Praxeas*, xxv.

14. Kelly, *Early Christian Doctrines*, p. 113, 114.

15. Roberts and Donaldson, *Ante-Nicene Fathers*, Vol. 3, p. 34, *Apology*, xxi.

16. Ibid., Vol. 3, p. 598, *Against Praxeas*, ii.

17. Ibid., Vol. 5, p. 151, *Refutation of All Heresies*, X, xxix.

18. Ibid., Vol. 5, p. 624, *Treatise Concerning the Trinity*, XV.

19. Ibid., Vol. 5, p. 620, *Treatise Concerning the Trinity*, XI.

20. Philip Schaff, *History of the Christian Church*, 8 vols. in 3 (Wilmington, Del.: Associated Publishers and Authors), Vol. 3 pp. 254, 255.

21. Roberts and Donaldson, *Ante-Nicene Fathers*, Vol. 4, pp. 245, 246, *de Principiis*, I. ii. 1.
22. Ibid., Vol. 4, p. 251, *de Principiis*, I. ii. 11.
23. Ibid., Vol. 4, p. 253, *de Principiis*, I. iii. 4.
24. Kelly, *Early Christian Doctrines*, p. 132, citing Origen, *de Principiis*, I. iii. 8.
25. Roberts and Donaldson, *Ante-Nicene Fathers*, Vol. 4, p. 255, *de Principiis*, I. iii. 7.
26. Ibid., Vol. 4, p. 247, *de Principiis*, I. ii. 4.
27. Ibid., Vol. 4, p. 249, *de Principiis*, I. ii. 8.
28. Ibid., Vol. 4, p. 250, *de Principiis*, I. ii. 10.
29. Ibid., Vol. 4, p. 255, *de Principiis*, I. iii. 7.
30. Philip Schaff, *Creeds of Christendom* (Grand Rapids: Baker, 1977, rpt.), Vol. 2, pp. 11-41 for this and the following creeds.
31. Ibid., Vol. 2, p. 28.
32. Rousas John Rushdoony, *The Foundations of Social Order: Studies in the Creeds and Councils of the Early Church* (Philadelphia: Presbyterian and Reformed, 1975), p. 13.

CHAPTER THREE

1. Schaff, *History of the Christian Church*, Vol. 3, p. 260.
2. Philip Schaff and Henry Wace, *Nicene and Post-Nicene Fathers* (Grand Rapids: Eerdmans, 1976 rpt.) Vol. 2, pp. 10, 11, in Socrates' *Ecclesiastical History*, I. 8.
3. Robert M. Grant, "Religion and Politics at the Council of Nicaea," *Journal of Religion*, 55 (Jan. 1975) p. 7.
4. Kelly, *Early Christian Doctrines*, p. 233.
5. Schaff, *History of the Christian Church*, Vol. 3, pp. 272, 273.
6. Schaff, *Creeds of Christendom*, Vol. 1, pp. 28, 29.
7. Schaff and Wace, *Nicene and Post-Nicene Fathers*, Vol 2, pp. 10-12, in Socrates' *Ecclesiastical History*, I. 8.
8. *Schaff-Herzog*, s.v. "Arianism" by P. Schaff.
9. Schaff and Wace, *Nicene and Post-Nicene Fathers*, Vol. 2, p. 277, cited in Sozomen's *Ecclesiastical History*, ii. 27.
10. Kelly, *Early Christian Doctrines*, p. 238.
11. Schaff, *History of the Christian Church*, Vol. 3, p. 261.
12. Ibid.
13. Ibid., Vol. 3, p. 264.
14. Schaff and Wace, *Nicene and Post-Nicene Fathers*, Vol. 4, p. 385, *Against the Arians*, ii. 70.
15. Ibid., Vol. 4, p. 84.
16. Kelly, *Early Christian Doctrines*, p. 248.
17. Ibid., p. 250.

18. Louis Berkhof, *History of Christian Doctrines* (Carlisle, Pa.: Banner of Truth Trust, 1975), p. 85.
19. Schaff and Wace, *Nicene and Post-Nicene Fathers*, Vol. 4, pp. 484, 485, in *Tome to the Antiochenes*, 5, 6.
20. *Schaff-Herzog*, s.v. "Arianism," by P. Schaff.
21. Schaff, *History of the Christian Church*, Vol. 3, p. 263.
22. Ibid., p. 265.

CHAPTER FOUR

1. John H. Leith, ed., *Creeds of the Church*, revised ed. (Richmond, Va.: John Knox Press, 1973), p. 29.
2. Schaff, *History of the Christian Church*, Vol. 3, p. 269.